SUDAN'S
MARSHALL PLAN (SMP)

*Rebuilding the World's
Forgotten Powerhouse*

KAMIL IDRIS

Editing, design, typesetting and publishing by UK Book Publishing.

www.ukbookpublishing.com

ISBN: 978-1-917329-71-2

DEDICATION

To those whose wisdom and guidance have shaped this journey – your support and encouragement have been invaluable.

I extend my deepest gratitude to my wife, Azza, my daughter, Dahd, President Mauro Poggia, Ambassador Hassan Hamid, Dr Hussein El-Hafyan, Dr Salah Al-Bander, Ambassador Badreldin Elguaifri, Consul-General Dr Nasreldin Hamad Eltayeb, Consul-General Mr Nizar Abdallah and Dr Mustaffa Hamid.

Your generosity and insight have left an indelible mark on this work.

Above all, to the people of Sudan – this great nation.

CONTENTS

PROLOGUE

The Forgotten Powerhouse

The sun sets over the plains of Sudan, with golden hues on a land that holds untold riches beneath its soil and within its culture. A contradictory country: its land potentially could feed the world, although it's still threatened by hunger. A nation filled with fertile land, gold, water, minerals and oil, yet held down by poverty. A nation whose resilience has survived centuries of strife, yet their unity remains fragile. Sudan, a country most often seen through the lens of war, famine, and despair, it is also a place of beauty, civilization, strength and possibility.

For a long time, Sudan has been a battleground of ideologies, ethnic divides and external interests. Its history is marred by a brutal civil war, devastating conflicts in Darfur and other regions and the eventual secession of South Sudan. Millions have been displaced, lives shattered and dreams deferred. The scars of these events are etched deeply into the hearts of its people and the ruins of its cities. Yet, even amidst the rubble, there is a glimmer of substantial hope, a vision for a resurgent Sudan.

This book discusses the tragedies that have befallen Sudan. It is about revealing the immense potential that is untapped. Sudan is a great nation; it is about more than its wars. It has some of the most sought out, rare and needed resources in the world, with the capability of becoming the breadbasket of Africa and a major player worldwide in the field of global agriculture. The majestic Nile holds the promise of hydroelectric power and live-giving irrigation. Underneath the soil, there lies treasures of minerals, gold, oil and untapped resources. These resources could fuel a new era of prosperity. Sudan's extensive culture is shaped by ancient Nubian civilisations alongside a rich and diverse range of ethnic groups that offers a foundation for unity and deserved global recognition.

However, potential on its own isn't sufficient. Sudan is at a crossroads, between instability and a renaissance that could not only transform the nation, but the region as well. What Sudan needs right now is a strategic, bold plan. A roadmap that both reimagines what it can become, while simultaneously rebuilding what has been destroyed. This is where Sudan's "Marshall Plan" comes in – it is inspired by the post-World War II reconstruction of Europe initiated by George Marshall, the then US Secretary of State. As Europe was before, Sudan now requires ambitious, comprehensive and coordinated effort to rebuild and heal its divisions while harnessing great untapped potential.

The Marshall Plan for Sudan is not simply a dream; it is a necessity. It is a call to action for Sudanese leaders, African and Arab neighbours as well as the global community. The plan focuses on the immense resources as the framework of recovery, empowerment of women and youth as drivers of change, as well as fostering good governance towards the cornerstone of stability. It is all about rebuilding the infrastructure, roads, railways, schools and hospitals while building trust among a fractured people. It is about making a powerhouse out of Sudan, not only for its nation, but for the world. It is a nation too rich in resources, history, and talent to be a forgotten one.

A new dawn awaits on the horizon, as the sun sets on Sudan. The story of a nation poised for rebirth, a group of people ready to rise from the ashes, and of a plan that could thrive and prosper. The question is not whether Sudan would rise again, it is whether the world should join in making it happen.

This book is the blueprint for that future, and the journey starts here.

INTRODUCTION

Why Sudan Matters

S udan is one of the richest nations in Africa in terms of natural resources. However, it suffered from some difficult economic collapses. While it relies on some food imports and international aid, it has abundant livestock and fertile lands it could fall back on instead. Due to the positioning of Sudan, it possesses immense geopolitical significance, but due to conflict, mismanagement, and external interferences, the nation's global affairs have been relegated to the sidelines.

Sudan's story is one that is filled with immense promise and so much tragedy. Once a thriving nation as the seat of ancient Nubian and Kushite civilizations. Home to pharaohs, scholars and merchants. A nation repeatedly brought down to its knees by war, and division. Sudan has been defined by civil wars, ethnic strife, and severe economic hardship. However, despite all that, the embers of significant hope still burn.

This book is not merely a documentation of Sudan's immense wealth nor its history of suffering. It is a blueprint for its revival, for a resurgent Sudan to rise from the ashes of war and economic strife towards becoming the epitome of stability, leadership and prosperity in Africa. "Marshall Plan for Sudan" is not about charity or foreign dependence, rather it is about a structured, deliberate strategy to bring forth the immense potential for the nation, heal the economy, and position it as a powerhouse in the 21st century.

Sudan, more than a troubled African nation, has great potential both as an economic leader and regional stability. Sharing the border with seven countries – South Sudan, Egypt, Libya, Chad, the Central African Republic, Ethiopia and Eritrea – in turn makes it a central player in regional trade, diplomacy and security.

The access Sudan has to the Red Sea gives it great geopolitical value. As global trades are heavily dependent on maritime routes, the ports of Sudan have potential to become major economic hubs. Although, instead of capitalizing, and taking advantage, Sudan has been sidelined and overshadowed by political instability and lack of effective infrastructure.

A Land of Untapped Wealth

Most of the underutilized resources in Africa are in Sudan.

1. Agriculture: Over 200 million hectares of most fertile soil and arable land. Access to the River Nile.
2. Potential to become a leading exporter of: wheat, sorghum, cotton, gum arabic and livestock, enabling it to become the breadbasket for the continent.
3. Mineral Wealth: Is home to deposits of gold, oil, copper and other valuable minerals. Gold accounts for billions in potential revenue yet much of it is extracted informally, smuggled out of the country, or exploited by foreign interests.
4. Water and Energy Resources: The River Nile is one of the major assets. It is a water source that could be multifaceted. It can be useful in agriculture, hydropower, and in the industry. Mismanagement

is the primary blame for the water shortages,
the electricity blackouts and lack of appropriate
irrigation systems. If planned properly, a strategy
could make Sudan an energy-independent nation,
and export electricity to neighbouring countries.

5. Human Capital: Sudan is home to a resilient young
population (60% under the age of 30) eager for
change. Has potential for economic transformation
if education, skills training and job creation were to
be put first.

The High Cost of Conflict and Neglect

Sudan has become a nation in need of foreign support, instead of becoming an agricultural and industrial powerhouse. A nation which, rather than leveraging its gold and oil reserves, sees much of that revenue disappear illegally or lost in conflict.

The consequences of this situation are devastating:

- People are facing food insecurity, despite the
agricultural potential of the nation.
- Children out of school as war and poverty rise.
- People are displaced due to the ongoing violence
and lack of stability.
- Crippling economy due to inflation and foreign
debt.

Contrary to what one might think, this is a global crisis rather than a national one. The recent instability of the country has been caused by the invasion of the Rapid Support Forces (RSF) and their accompanying militias recruited from all over the world. Such instability affects its neighbours, fuels refugee crises, and creates vulnerability to exploitation by extremist groups.

Sudan Marshall Plan:

A Blueprint for Renewal

As history has shown, post-conflict nations have risen from devastation before. Post-World War II, Europe's state was: shattered economies, broken infrastructure and millions displaced. The Marshall Plan's implementation stage was successful in rebuilding and modernizing Europe.

Sudan needs an approach that is relevant in terms of strategy, focused on long term reconstruction, the revival of the economy and institutional reform.

Four pillars for Sudan's Marshall Plan:

1. Economical transformation: Shift from aid-dependent economy to self-sustaining industrial and agricultural leader.
2. Governance and Rule of Law: Inclusive civilian government, anti-corruption and reformation of institutions.
3. Infrastructure and development: investing in railways, ports, energy, roads, for both internal and external connections.
4. Social rebuilding and human capital: Putting education, healthcare and job creation first, thus empowering the people of Sudan as drivers of progress.

This book will lay out a detailed roadmap for how Sudan can implement its own Marshall Plan. It will explore case studies from nations that have successfully rebuilt after war, highlight Sudan's economic potential, and provide actionable strategies for achieving sustainable development.

The Urgency of Now

This book is a call to action. It is for Sudanese leaders seeking a path forward, for international allies looking for ways to invest in Sudan's future, and for the Sudanese people themselves, who have suffered enough and deserve a nation that reflects their strength, resilience, and potential.

Sudan has all the ingredients for success. The question is: Will it seize this opportunity?

The next chapters will explore how Sudan can transition from crisis to prosperity, beginning with an honest look at its history, the impact of conflict, and the roadblocks that must be overcome to build a resurgent Sudan. One that is not defined by war, but by growth, stability, and leadership. The journey begins now.

CHAPTER 1

A HISTORY OF GREATNESS AND GRIEF

T he history of Sudan is a testament to the depths of human suffering and the heights of civilization. A nation of ancient kingdoms that once upon a time flourished. Culture and trade routes were intersected and some of the greatest historical achievements in Africa were made in Sudan. Sudan also endured centuries of colonization, exploitation, division and conflict. To fully understand Sudan's present, and its potential, history must be studied first.

Long before the borders of Sudan were drawn, some of Africa's most advanced civilizations lived there. The Kingdom of Kush ruled many territories along the Nile. The capital Meroë (Merawi) became the centre of trade, technological advancements and wealth. They built more than 200 pyramids, outnumbering the Egyptian pyramids. This created a powerful empire thriving on commerce, military conquests and iron smelting.

The ancient civilizations were known for many things, including their military strength, contributions to architecture, to culture, and to governance. The Nubian pharaohs of Kush ruled Egypt and formed the 25th Dynasty of the Egyptian Empire. Sudan linked the Mediterranean world with sub-Saharan Africa. The Sudanese people played a vital role in the exchange of goods, technology, and ideas.

Sudan's rich history and great nation have been destabilized by disruption to their internal communities and foreign domination.

By the 19th century, the nation was caught in the crosshairs of foreign powers. Sudan was exploited by the Ottoman empire and the rule of the Egyptians. Exploitation was not limited to resources, it included people as slavery, gold, and ivory. In 1899 the Anglo-Egyptian Condominium was created, bringing the nation under colonial ruling.

Independence and the Struggle for Unity

In 1956, Sudan's independence was met with celebration yet filled with uncertainty. Colonial rulers caused a fragile state. It left the institutions weak, internal divisions, and unresolved questions of identity and governance.

A year after gaining independence, Sudan's first civil war between North and South broke out from 1955-1972.

The Darfur Genocide and the International Response

Even as Sudan was dealing with the fallout of the civil war, another devastating conflict erupted in Darfur in 2003. The Sudanese government, accused of systematically targetting ethnic African communities in the region, backed brutal militia groups known as the Janjaweed. The result was a humanitarian catastrophe – villages were burned, thousands of women were raped, and an estimated 300,000 people were killed. Millions were displaced, many fleeing into refugee camps in Chad and other neighbouring countries.

Military Coups and Political Instability

Sudan's history since independence has been marred by a cycle of military coups and failed governance. From General Ibrahim Abboud's coup in 1958 to Jaafar Nimeiry's rule in the 1970s and 80s, military leaders have repeatedly seized power, promising reform but delivering modest development.

In 1989, Omar al-Bashir staged a military coup and ruled Sudan for 30 years. Despite discovery of oil and years of positive development, his regime was accused of human rights violations, and escalation of the war in Darfur.

In 2018–2019, mass protests erupted across the country, fuelled by economic crises and public frustration. In April 2019, al-Bashir was finally overthrown by the military after months of relentless protests led by young people and women. Sudan's struggle was far from over.

The 2019 Revolution and the Path to Democracy

Following al-Bashir's ousting, Sudan entered a period of political transition. A civilian-military power-sharing agreement was established, raising hopes for a new era of democracy. Instability of the country continued. To make things worse, on the 15th of April, the Rapid Support Forces (RSF) instigated a failed military coup followed by an internal devastating war that continued until the time of writing of this plan. RSF committed war crimes and crimes against humanity.

Despite these setbacks, Sudanese activists, civil society groups, and ordinary citizens continue to fight for democracy. The December Revolution of 2019 showed the world that Sudan's people are resilient, determined, and capable of shaping their own destiny. The ongoing struggle for a civilian-led government is a testament to their unwavering spirit.

The Road to Renewal

Sudan's history has been a blend of both triumph and tragedy. It is a nation that has produced great civilizations, rich cultures, and untapped resources, yet it has also suffered from colonization, division, war, and dictatorship. The weight of history has been heavy, but it does not have to define Sudan's future.

The lessons of the past are clear: Sudan cannot afford to remain trapped in cycles of violence and mismanagement. The road to renewal must be built on national unity, inclusive governance, economic development, and a commitment to justice and reconciliation. Sudan has the potential to become a leading nation in Africa and the world, one that is stable, prosperous, and a key player in global affairs.

This book will lay out the blueprint for that transformation. The next chapter will explore the devastating cost of Sudan's conflicts, not just in terms of lives lost but also in the economic and social destruction that has held the country back. Understanding these consequences is essential to forging a new path forward, one that ensures Sudan's past does not dictate its future.

CHAPTER 2

THE COST OF CONFLICT

S udan has experienced two of Africa's longest and deadliest civil wars. It is a nation that has been defined by war, political instability and hardship. The Darfur war and other conflicts have displaced millions and devastated the economy. The consequences of this fall not only in the cities and villages, they also affect society, education, healthcare, governance and economic development.

Sudan's struggles are a product of decades of wrong governance, ethnic divisions and failure to establish an identity that includes the Sudanese people as a whole, as well as a national project. The cost of conflict is measured not solely based on lost opportunities, to build, grow and lead, but also on lives lost. To understand the urgency of Sudan's reconstruction, we must first examine the devastating consequences of its past conflicts.

The Human Toll: A Nation in Mourning

The wars in Sudan have left millions of people displaced, dead or permanently scarred. The first civil war (1955-1972) took the lives of over half a million people. The second civil war (1983-2005) was even worse, resulting in the war being one of the deadliest in modern history.

In 2003, the war in Darfur began; the Sudanese government used janjaweed militias to crush rebellion. This led to one of the worst humanitarian crises. Families were separated, women were subjected to sexual violence, and villages were burnt to the ground.

Even after the secession of South Sudan in 2011, the conflicts in Blue Nile and South Kordofan continued to claim lives. The military's response to pro-democracy movements in 2019 and 2021 demonstrated that violence remains a tool of political control.

Beyond numbers, the personal stories that are told are even worse. Mothers losing their children, young people never having a chance to resume school, farmers, whose lands were completely destroyed. Each one is a reminder that war doesn't only happen on the battlefield. The consequences linger on for decades, passed on, from one generation to the other.

Economic Devastation: A Nation Robbed of Its Wealth

The conflicts in Sudan and the current war, triggered by the Rapid Support Forces (RSF), have not only taken lives, they have also crippled the economy. In the 1950s and 1960s. Sudan was one of the most promising economies in Africa. Decades of war and mismanagement led to this economic foundation, leaving the nation impoverished.

The Second Civil War cost billions of dollars for Sudan. This led to lost productivity, infrastructure destruction and military spending. Industries collapsed, trade routes were severed, and farms were abandoned completely. The war with South Sudan also led to the loss of oil revenues.

The aftermath and impact of the ongoing war is still felt today, especially economically. Inflation spiralled out of control, foreign investment is non-existent, and unemployment is at large. Sudan is rich in natural resources; however, its inability to politically stabilize has created a challenge to capitalize on these assets.

The Social Fabric Torn Apart

The most damaging legacy of Sudan's conflicts is the division that has been created within the country. Wars have been fought not just over land and resources, but also over identity. These conflicts reinforced ethnic and regional divisions, thus making unity a challenging goal.

This made it difficult to build a strong national identity. Leaders have exploited ethnic and religious differences to maintain power, rather than working towards unity. The result is a nation where trust between communities is extremely fragile and where peace agreements are broken.

The displacement of millions has only worsened these divisions. Refugee camps, meant to be temporary, have become permanent homes for entire generations. The longer people remain displaced, the harder it becomes for them to reintegrate into society.

The Collapse of Education and Healthcare

The wars have also impacted education and the healthcare system, creating lack of access to basic services. Schools were bombed, teachers fled, children were recruited as soldiers rather than being given an education.

The lack of education has long-term consequences. Without a well-educated population, Sudan struggles to build a skilled workforce, attract investment, and develop a modern economy.

Education is not only about literacy, it is also about the need for innovation, governance, and economic growth. Sudan's failure to invest in its youth has left it with a workforce that is underprepared for the challenges of the 21st century.

Sudan's healthcare system has been neglected for decades. Hospitals lack basic supplies, doctors are underpaid, and millions of Sudanese rely on underfunded public clinics that cannot meet demand. During times of war, healthcare infrastructure is often deliberately targeted, leaving war-affected regions without access to medical treatment. The result is high rates of maternal and infant mortality, the spread of preventable diseases, and a life expectancy that lags behind global averages.

The Global Consequences of Sudan's Conflicts

Sudan's instability does not exist in isolation; it has regional and global repercussions. Millions of Sudanese refugees have fled to neighbouring countries, straining the resources of nations like Chad, Egypt, Ethiopia, and South Sudan. The conflict has also fuelled arms smuggling, human trafficking, and extremist activities in the region, making Sudan a focal point of global security concerns.

The economic impact of Sudan's instability extends beyond its borders. The country's vast agricultural potential remains untapped, affecting global food markets. Its Red Sea ports, which could serve as major trade hubs, remaining underdeveloped due to political instability. If Sudan were to achieve stability and economic growth, it could become a key player in regional and international trade and development.

The True Cost of Conflict: A Nation Held Hostage

The cost of conflict is not just what Sudan has lost, it is what it has failed to become. But history has shown that nations can rise from the ruins of war. Germany and Japan were devastated by World War II but rebuilt themselves into economic powerhouses. Rwanda, after the 1994 genocide, transformed itself into one of Africa's most stable and fast-growing economies. Sudan, too, can rebuild.

The question is: Will Sudan seize the opportunity to break free from its cycle of conflict?

The next chapter will explore Sudan's vast but underutilized resources: the riches buried beneath the soil, the fertile lands left uncultivated, and the human capital waiting to be mobilized. The true cost of war is the wasted potential of a nation, but the promise of peace is the chance to finally realize it.

Current War in Sudan

The current war in Sudan began on the 15th of April 2023, was the start of a brutal conflict initiated by the Rapid Support Forces (RSF). The RSF launched a surprise attack against the Sudanese Armed Forces (SAF) at key military and government sites in Khartoum.

The RSF has committed so many grave atrocities, including, but not limited to, mass killings, ethnic cleansing, sexual violence, and looting, particularly targeting civilians throughout the country.

Reports from different organizations and the United Nations confirm war crimes and crimes against humanity. The entire Sudan is displaced especially in areas where the RSF and allied militias have perpetrated genocidal violence against the Masalit people.

This war has led to a humanitarian crisis. Famine is looming and the healthcare system has collapsed. The RSF's brutal ethnic targeting caused the destruction of the entire country.

CHAPTER 3

BURIED RICHES, SUDAN'S UNTAPPED POTENTIAL

S udan's riches remain ignored, mismanaged, buried or exploited for the benefit of a select few rather than their nation. While Sudan is often associated with war and economic collapse, its immense potential should be highly recognized. Sudan is not a poor country; it is a country whose wealth has yet to be fully realized. Its fertile lands, abundant water sources, vast mineral reserves, and strategic geographic location make it one of the most resource-rich nations in Africa and globally. Yet, instead of becoming an economic powerhouse, the nation remains trapped in cycles of invisibility and underdevelopment.

This chapter will explore the hidden wealth of Sudan, its agricultural potential, mineral resources, water reserves and human capital. These assets, if properly utilized, could transform the country into a thriving economic hub.

Sudan as Africa's Breadbasket

Sudan, possessing over 200 million hectares of land, makes it one of the most agriculturally blessed nations on Earth. This country has the potential to become the breadbasket of Africa, capable of feeding and exporting food to the region and beyond. The Nile River, along with rainfall, provides Sudan with water supply that could sustain year-round agriculture, if managed appropriately.

Sudan was a major producer of cotton, wheat, gum arabic, sorghum, and sesame. In the 1970s, Sudan's Gezira Scheme was one of the largest and most successful irrigation projects in Africa. This transformed thousands of hectares of land into farmland. Mismanagement and a lack of modernization caused the agricultural sector to dramatically decline.

The failure to develop Sudan's agriculture is a national security risk. A country that cannot feed itself remains vulnerable. This could lead to external pressures and further instability. Agricultural exports could generate billions in revenue, provide employment for millions and reduce poverty. There needs to be investment in irrigation systems, modern supply chains, mechanized farming, then perhaps, Sudan could reclaim itself as a leading food producer in Africa.

To achieve this, Sudan must prioritize land reform, support small farmers with access to credit and modern technology, and attract investment in agribusiness. If Sudan harnesses even a fraction of its agricultural potential, it could transform its economy and ensure food security for generations to come.

Sudan's Hidden Treasure: The Wealth Beneath the Soil

Sudan is a country that is the most mineral-rich in Africa. With deposits of gold, copper, oil, and rare minerals that are all underdeveloped or exploited through informal and illegal channels.

- Gold: 93 tons of Gold is extracted annually. It is the third largest producer of gold in Africa. Much of this gold is mined and smuggled out of Sudan; 80% of Sudan's gold bypasses the formal economy. With investment and proper regulation, in mining technology and transparency in the management of revenue, the gold industry could fund national development.
- Oil: South Sudan was the primary source of oil before the secession in 2011. The South then took the majority of oil fields. Improving the oil refining infrastructure would help Sudan regain some of the lost energy revenue.
- Copper, Uranium and Rare Minerals: Sudan is believed to have large reserves of copper, uranium and rare minerals that are critical for the global technology industry. Political instability and lack of political survey have caused the resources to remain untapped. If Sudan's mining sector is managed and developed responsibly, it could become the top supplier for essential minerals for global markets.

The way to unlock Sudan's mineral wealth is regulation and transparency. Historically, corruption has plagued the mining sectors with both foreign interests or elites, always benefiting at the expense of Sudan's people. If strict oversight and ensuring fair revenue distribution was done, it could make sure that these resources contribute to national development rather than being siphoned away.

Water and Energy: The Power of the Nile

Sudan has access to one of the world's most important rivers, the Nile. The country has the potential to develop hydroelectric power, to expand irrigation and ensure clean water for all of Sudan.

- Hydroelectric Power: Sudan has several hydroelectric dams, including the Merowe Dam, which has significantly increased the energy production of the country. Full potential of hydro resources remains underutilized. Sudan could not only generate, but export energy to neighbouring countries, if further investment was given.

Water Management for Agriculture: While Sudan has significant water access, the outdated infrastructure and modest irrigation systems mean that much of this water is wasted. Modernization of Sudan's irrigation networks could increase agricultural yields, reducing dependence on rain-fed farming.

- Solar and renewable energy: Sudan has one of the highest solar energy potentials in Africa. With around 300 sunny days a year, Sudan could invest in large scale solar farms. This would reduce their reliance on expensive diesel imports and outdated power grids, and provide affordable sustainable electricity.

By prioritizing sustainable energy and water management, Sudan can reduce its dependence on fossil fuels, lower production costs, and create a more stable economic foundation.

Human Capital: The Untapped Workforce

Sudan's most valuable asset is its people. More than half of the population is under the age of 30. Sudan has a young, dynamic workforce that could drive innovation and economic growth.

– Education Reform: The educational system must be prioritized with regards to rebuilding. Children must have access to quality schooling. STEM investments could be preparing Sudan's youth for jobs in emerging industries.

Vocational Training and Job Creation: Technical and vocational training can equip young people with essential skills needed for manufacturing, construction and modern agriculture.

– Entrepreneurship and innovation: Sudanese entrepreneurs could build local industries, reducing reliance on imports and creating a self-sustaining economy.

A nation's future is determined by the strength of its workforce. By investing in its people, Sudan can build a skilled, resilient population capable of transforming the country from the inside out.

– Culture industries: With the richness of Sudan's diversified culture, folklore and genetic resources, Sudan could be a major hub for renewed culture industries worldwide. This sector alone could be a catalyst in the financial performance of the country.

A Nation on the Brink of Opportunity

Sudan is not poor. All the resources needed to become a thriving, self-sufficient nation, Sudan has at its disposal. For decades, these riches have remained buried, ignored, underdeveloped, or mismanaged. The tragedy of Sudan is not that it lacks wealth, but that it has failed to use it wisely, effectively and efficiently.

The next chapter will explore the lessons Sudan can learn from other countries that have risen from conflict before. From post-war Europe's Marshall Plan to Rwanda's economic transformation, Sudan has examples to follow. The question is not whether Sudan can rebuild, but how it will choose to use its immense potential. The time for waiting is over. Sudan's resources must now be put to work for the benefit of its people.

CHAPTER 4

LESSONS FROM THE MARSHALL PLAN REBUILDING A NATION FROM THE ASHES

History has demonstrated that nations can rise from the destruction of war, economic collapse and social disintegration. After World War II, Europe was reduced to rubble, the economy shattered and people were displaced. Now, Europe has rebuilt itself into a Global Economic Powerhouse. This was achieved by a strategic well-funded, internationally coordinated effort known as the Marshall Plan.

Sudan stands at a critical juncture. After years of political instability, it was left impoverished and struggling to regain stability. However, we know from history, recovery is possible. This chapter explores how the Marshall Plan can serve as a blueprint for Sudan's reconstruction. By learning from history, Sudan can forge a path towards sustainable growth and stability.

What Was the Marshall Plan?

Europe faced a humanitarian and economic catastrophe following World War II. Industries were destroyed, millions were on the brink of starvation, and infrastructure was in ruins. The United States realized that if Europe collapsed, this would create a humanitarian crisis and fuel political extremism. Due to this, in 1946, the US introduced the Marshall Plan, which was a large economic aid programme designed to rebuild war-stricken economies, restore political stability and modernize industries.

This plan was officially referred to as the "European Recovery Program (ERP)" and provided over 13 billion USD in financial aid to 16 Western European countries. These were the goals outlined:

1. Rebuilding infrastructure: roads, bridges, housing and factories were reconstructed to restore normal life and economic activity.
2. Modernizing industry: Outdated processes were all upgraded to boost efficiency and productivity.
3. Stabilizing Economies: New financial institutions were created; trade was stabilized to create economic integration.
4. Preventing Future Conflicts: Economic cooperation between European countries aided towards building the foundation for lasting peace, what later became known as the "European Union".

Within a decade, European economies had recovered, industry was booming, and political stability had returned to much of the region. The Marshall Plan is widely regarded as one of the most successful post-war reconstruction efforts in history.

Could Sudan implement a similar programme to rebuild its war-torn economy and fractured society? The answer is yes, but with adaptations to suit Sudan's unique challenges.

Lessons from the Marshall Plan for Sudan's Reconstruction

While the situation in Sudan is different from post-war Europe, the core principles of the Marshall Plan are still very relevant. Sudan doesn't require temporary relief nor does it require short-term aid. It requires a comprehensive national recovery plan of action.

Below are the five key lessons Sudan can take from the Marshall Plan to design its own National Reconstruction Plan.

Lesson 1: Investing in Infrastructure to Rebuild the Nation

One of the first priorities of the Marshall Plan was physical reconstruction. Without roads, bridges, ports, and power grids, economic recovery wouldn't be possible.

Sudan's infrastructure problems are immense:

- Roads and Transport: Many roads remain unpaved, making transportation slow. A lack of connectivity limits trade and economic growth.
- Energy and Electricity: Frequent power outages and inadequate energy distribution makes it difficult for industries to operate efficiently.
- Water and Sanitation: Millions of Sudanese lack access to clean water, and weak sanitation systems contribute to health crises.
- Telecommunications and Digital Infrastructure: Modern economies thrive on internet access and telecommunications; however, much of Sudan remains digitally disconnected.

A Sudanese Marshall Plan must focus on large-scale infrastructure projects that create jobs, attract investment, and integrate Sudan into regional and global markets. This means:

- Expanding road and railway networks to connect rural areas with major economic centres.
- Investing in renewable energy, including solar and hydroelectric power, to ensure stable electricity supply.
- Modernizing ports and logistics hubs to increase trade efficiency.
- Developing irrigation systems to support year-round agriculture.

A well-built infrastructure is the backbone of any thriving economy. Without it, no real progress can be made.

Lesson 2: Economic Stabilization and Modernization

One of the Marshall Plan's key achievements was restoring economic stability by:

- Controlling inflation and stabilizing currency.
- Attracting foreign investment.
- Reviving industries through modernization.

Sudan's economy remains fragile due to hyperinflation, a weak financial sector, and heavy reliance on informal markets. To stabilize its economy, Sudan must:

- Reform its banking sector to restore trust and increase access to credit.
- Attract foreign investment by ensuring transparency and reducing bureaucratic hurdles.
- Diversify its economy beyond agriculture and raw material exports, investing in manufacturing and technology.
- Control inflation through monetary policies and fiscal discipline.

A stable economy encourages long-term investment and creates a foundation for sustainable growth.

Lesson 3: Strengthening Institutions and Good Governance

Post-war Europe succeeded in rebuilding largely because of strong institutions and transparent governance. Sudan has long suffered from corruption, political instability, and weak institutions that fail to serve its people.

A Sudanese Marshall Plan must prioritize:

- Judicial and legal reforms to uphold the rule of law and fight corruption.
- Decentralization of governance to empower local communities.
- Public sector reform to ensure efficiency and accountability in government spending.
- Strengthening anti-corruption mechanisms to prevent the misuse of public funds.

No amount of foreign aid or investment will succeed if governance remains weak. Sudan must build institutions that protect, not exploit, its people.

Lesson 4: Regional Cooperation and Trade

One of the great successes of the Marshall Plan was fostering economic cooperation among European nations, laying the foundation for the European Union. Sudan can learn from this by strengthening regional trade and diplomatic partnerships.

- Expanding trade with neighbours like Egypt, Ethiopia, and South Sudan to create economic interdependence.
- Investing in regional transport corridors to facilitate movement of goods.
- Building economic agreements with African and Arab nations to secure markets for Sudanese products.

Sudan should not isolate itself, it must embrace its role as a regional economic leader.

Lesson 5: Investing in Human Capital

Europe's recovery was not just about rebuilding infrastructure; it was about empowering people through education and workforce development. Sudan must prioritize:

- Expanding education access to ensure literacy and technical skills for its youth.

- Vocational training programmes to build a skilled workforce in key industries.
- Encouraging entrepreneurship to foster local businesses, inventions and innovations. In this respect, the intellectual property system in the country should be reformed.
- Creating jobs in key sectors like agriculture, manufacturing, and technology.

A well-educated and skilled population is Sudan's greatest asset. Without investing in people, no economic recovery can be sustained.

Conclusion: The Urgency of Sudan's Reconstruction

The Marshall Plan transformed a war-torn Europe into an economic powerhouse. Sudan, despite its challenges, has the potential to follow a similar path. But time is running out. Sudan cannot afford another decade of stagnation and missed opportunities.

The Sudanese Marshall Plan must be bold, ambitious, and strategic. It must prioritize infrastructure, economic stability, governance reform, regional cooperation, and human capital development. The road to recovery is not easy, but history has shown that nations can rebuild, no matter how devastated they are.

The next chapter will outline a detailed plan for how Sudan can implement these strategies and begin its journey toward renewal. The time for action is now.

CHAPTER 5

BUILDING A UNIFIED NATION OVERCOMING DIVISION FOR A STRONGER SUDAN

A lack of resources has never been the issue in Sudan, nor is the issue economic potential nor strategic location. The issue is its inability to create and maintain a united national identity that goes beyond ethnicity, religion and regional divisions. For years, Sudan has been plagued by conflicts rooted in history and in economic inequality.

Sudan cannot become strong nor stable without addressing the deep-seated conflicts of divisions. The goal of a lasting reconstruction plan must be national unity and a national project. Without social unity and cohesion, no amount of foreign assistance, infrastructure development or economic investment will help.

The Root Causes of Sudan's Divisions

To understand how Sudan can achieve unity, it is essential to examine the historical factors that have kept the nation divided:

1. Ethnic and Regional Inequalities
   Sudan is one of the most ethnically diverse nations, over 500 ethnic groups and more than 100 languages spoken across the nation.

   This imbalance has fuelled resentment and led to repeated armed uprisings. The people of Darfur, the Nuba Mountains, and the Blue Nile have long felt neglected, receiving little investment in infrastructure, education, and healthcare. This systematic situation has driven these regions to seek autonomy or rebel against the central government.

2. The Legacy of Colonial Rule
   The colonial rule aggregated Sudan's divisions by governing South and North separately. The British colonization was enforcing policies that widened cultural and economic disparities.

3. Political Manipulation and Sectarianism
   Some of the successive Sudanese governments have used ethnic and religious identities as political tools, favouring certain groups while marginalizing others. Instead of fostering national unity, Sudanese leaders have often relied on a "divide and rule" strategy, making national integration even more difficult.

4. Unequal Distribution of Resources
   Many of Sudan's conflicts have been driven by disputes over land, water, and wealth distribution. The central government's control over oil revenues, agricultural land, and gold mines has led to deep

resentment among local communities who feel exploited and excluded from the country's wealth.

The Cost of a Divided Sudan

Sudan's failure to achieve unity has had devastating consequences:

- Prolonged conflicts: The country has spent more time at war than at peace, consuming national resources and preventing development.
- Economic stagnation: Political instability deters investment, weakens institutions, and stifles economic growth.
- Humanitarian crises: Millions of Sudanese have been displaced due to ethnic violence, creating ongoing humanitarian challenges.
- Global isolation: Sudan's instability has led to international sanctions, reputational damage, and loss of foreign partnerships.

A divided Sudan cannot prosper. Without national unity, any efforts to rebuild the country will be fragile and unsustainable.

Strategies for National Reconciliation and Unity

In order for Sudan to be a stronger and more unified country it must take steps towards healing past trauma. Sudan should ensure inclusivity and foster a shared national identity.

Below are important pillars of a national reconciliation and unity strategy:

1. Establishing a Truth, justice and reconciliation commission
   One of the best ways to heal a nation that has been divided is through truth and reconciliation. Sudan must come to terms with its history of war, oppression and human rights violations in an open and transparent manner. A national truth, justice and reconciliation commission like the one implemented in South Africa could allow victims to share their experience, hold perpetrators accountable and forge a path towards healing.
   The commission must:
   - Investigate past conflicts and the crimes committed.
   - Provide reparations to those who have suffered injustice.
   - Rebuild trust in order to facilitate a dialogue between communities.
   - Ensure that those responsible for the atrocities, face justice.

2. Power sharing and inclusive governance
   The true unification of Sudan will only take place if an inclusive governance model that represents all ethnic and regional groups is adopted. If a governance system is present, and it reflects the diversity of Sudan, it will definitely build confidence and reduce marginalization.
   The way to achieve this is by:
   - A decentralized system of governance that allows greater autonomy to regional governments.

- Reflecting the diversity in Sudan through political appointments.
- Empowerment of communities to take decisions about their own developments into their own hands.

3. National Identity and Cultural Integration
Sudan must move beyond sectarian divisions in order to build a mutual national identity. In order to achieve this: Sudanese people must see themselves as one nation.

- Education must be reformed to demonstrate Sudan's history, unity and common heritage.
- There must be national service aid programmes that bring people together.
- Cultural exchanges should be promoted through art, music, literature that demonstrates Sudan's diversity while reinforcing national unity. In this way diversity becomes an asset and not a liability.

4. Equitable Economic Development
For unification in Sudan to exist, all regions must thrive. Economic inclusion is an important pillar in national stability. The government must:

- Invest in the historically neglected sectors, such as infrastructure, education and healthcare.
- Ensure that all natural resources revenues benefit all regions.
- Plan and implement national projects that create economic opportunities for job markets in marginalized areas.

When all Sudanese feel they have an economic stake in the country's future, national unity becomes much stronger.

5. Conflict Resolution and Disarmament
   Armed militias remain a major threat to the
   stability of the country. Sudan has been flooded
   with weapons for years. The reintegration and
   disarmament of former fighters is necessary for
   long-term peace:
   – A community-based disarmament programme,
     allowing people to give up their weapons.
     These programmes would have an economic
     incentive.
   – Vocational training and skills training for ex-
     combatants, to transition into civilian life and
     join society.
   – Strengthening the security sector.

Without demilitarization, Sudan will remain vulnerable
to recurring violence.

The Path Forward: A Nation That Stands Together

Sudan's history has been full of divisions. The future
doesn't have to follow the same fate. If leaders and citizens
both commit to reconciliation, inclusive government and
equitable development, Sudan can break free from this cycle
of conflict and instability.

Creating national unity will be a challenge, it will require
compromise, courage and a strong willingness to confront
uncomfortable truths. However, without unity, the dream of
Sudan's economic recovery and global leadership is out of reach.

The next chapter will explore how to leverage Sudan's
agricultural potential for economic renewal. National unity
is the cornerstone of Sudan's future, and it must begin now.

CHAPTER 6

ECONOMIC REVIVAL AGRICULTURE AS THE BACKBONE OF SUDAN'S FUTURE

D ecades of instability, war, and neglect have left Sudan's agricultural sector underdeveloped, unable to fulfil its potential as the driver of economic growth. If Sudan is to rebuild, agriculture must be at the heart of its economic revival. A strong agricultural base can provide employment, reduce poverty, attract investment, and serve as a foundation for industrialization.

This chapter explores Sudan's untapped agricultural potential, the challenges that have prevented its growth, and the key strategies needed to transform it into a pillar of national prosperity.

Sudan's Agricultural Potential: A Sleeping Giant

Sudan's geographical and natural advantages make it one of the most promising agricultural nations in the world:

1. Vast Fertile Land: Sudan has one of the largest expanses of land in Africa, yet only a fraction is currently being cultivated.
2. The Nile and Seasonal Rainfall: The Nile provides a consistent water source for irrigation, while Sudan's diverse climate zones allow for a wide variety of crops.
3. Livestock Production: Sudan is home to millions of cattle, sheep, goats, and camels, making it a key player in Africa's livestock industry.
4. Strategic Location: Sudan's position between Africa and the Middle East makes it an ideal agricultural exporter to Gulf countries and North Africa.

In theory, Sudan should be one of the richest agricultural nations in the world. But in reality, its agricultural sector is in decline, failing to meet even the basic needs of its people.

Why Sudan's Agricultural Sector Has Failed

Despite its natural wealth, Sudan's agriculture has suffered from years of neglect. The main obstacles include:

1. Lack of Modernization and Infrastructure
   - Outdated farming techniques and lack of mechanization reduce productivity.
   - Poor irrigation systems lead to water waste and inconsistent crop yields.
   - A lack of roads and storage facilities makes it difficult for farmers to transport goods to markets, leading to food loss and higher prices.

2. Government Neglect and Corruption
   - Agricultural policies have been inconsistent, often prioritizing cash crops for export rather than food security.
   - Government control over agricultural projects has led to inefficiency and mismanagement.
   - Corrupt land distribution practices have deprived small farmers of opportunities, benefiting political elites instead.
3. Impact of War and Political Instability
   - Armed conflicts in key agricultural regions (Darfur, South Kordofan, Blue Nile) have displaced farmers and disrupted food production.
   - Sanctions and economic isolation have limited access to modern technology and foreign investment.
   - The lack of secure land rights has discouraged investment in long-term agricultural projects.
4. Climate Change and Environmental Challenges
   - Increasing desertification threatens fertile lands.
   - Rising temperatures and erratic rainfall make traditional farming methods unreliable.
   - Poor land management has led to soil degradation, reducing long-term productivity.

If Sudan does not address these challenges, it will continue to struggle with food insecurity, economic stagnation, and rural poverty.

A Roadmap for Agricultural Revival

To unlock Sudan's full agricultural potential, a comprehensive national strategy is needed. Below are the key steps Sudan must take to transform its agricultural sector into a pillar of economic stability.

1. Large-Scale Investment in Irrigation and Infrastructure
    Sudan's reliance on seasonal rainfall makes its agriculture highly vulnerable to climate change. To ensure consistent food production, the government must:
    -   Expand irrigation networks, using the Nile and underground water sources to provide year-round farming.
    -   Modernize water management systems to reduce waste and improve efficiency.
    -   Build roads and storage facilities to connect rural farmers to markets, reducing food loss and transportation costs. Investment in infrastructure will increase productivity, stabilize food prices, and make Sudan's agriculture more competitive globally.
2. Agricultural Mechanization and Technology Adoption
    Many Sudanese farmers still rely on traditional farming methods, leading to low crop yields and high labour costs. The introduction of modern technology can dramatically improve efficiency.
    -   Providing farmers with access to tractors, irrigation pumps, and modern equipment will increase productivity.

- Using satellite and data-driven farming techniques can help predict weather patterns and optimize planting schedules.
- Training programmes for farmers in modern agricultural methods will improve efficiency and crop yields.

Countries like India and Brazil successfully modernized their agriculture through technological investment, resulting in massive economic gains. Sudan must follow suit.

3. Land Reform and Rural Development
   For agriculture to thrive, fair and transparent land policies are essential. Sudan's land ownership system has long been dominated by government elites and foreign investors, leaving many small farmers without secure land rights.
   - Implementing land ownership reforms will give farmers legal security and encourage investment in long-term projects.
   - Providing financial incentives and loans to small farmers will help increase production.
   - Developing rural infrastructure (schools, hospitals, markets) will encourage people to stay in farming communities rather than migrating to overcrowded cities. Secure land ownership empowers farmers, making them invest more in their land and increase food production.

4. Strengthening Local and Regional Markets
   Sudan must prioritize domestic food security before focusing on exports. This means:
   - Supporting local food markets instead of prioritizing large-scale cash crop exports.

- Encouraging cooperatives where small farmers can pool resources and sell collectively.
- Reducing reliance on food imports by boosting local production. Once food security is achieved, Sudan can then expand exports to neighbouring countries and global markets.

5. Investing in Livestock and Agro-Processing Industries

Sudan has one of the largest livestock populations in Africa. However, most of its meat and dairy products are exported raw, without value addition.

- Investing in meat processing plants, dairy farms, and leather industries can significantly increase profits.
- Developing cold storage facilities will allow Sudan to export high-quality meat products to the Gulf and Europe.
- Promoting sustainable livestock management will reduce overgrazing and protect the environment. Instead of exporting raw materials, Sudan must process its agricultural products locally, creating jobs and boosting industrialization.

6. Attracting Investment and International Partnerships

To finance these reforms, Sudan must attract investment from:

- Private sector companies interested in agricultural development.
- International organizations like the World Bank and African Development Bank.
- Regional partners such as Egypt, the UAE, and Saudi Arabia, which are interested in securing food supplies.

However, Sudan must ensure that foreign investments benefit local farmers rather than exploit them. Deals must be transparent, sustainable, and mutually beneficial.

A Future Built on Agriculture

Sudan's economic future lies in its land. A well-developed agricultural sector can:

- Provide millions of jobs, reducing unemployment and rural poverty.
- Ensure food security, eliminating hunger and reducing reliance on imports.
- Drive industrial growth, as food processing, textiles, and livestock industries expand.
- Boost exports, increasing foreign exchange reserves and strengthening the economy.

If Sudan prioritizes agriculture, it can emerge as a leader in Africa's food production and economic development.

The next chapter will focus on Sudan's mineral wealth, exploring how the country can responsibly harness its gold, oil, and other natural resources to build a sustainable and diversified economy. Sudan must look beyond raw exports and toward value-added industries that creates long-term prosperity.

CHAPTER 7

UNLOCKING SUDAN'S MINERAL WEALTH A PATH TO ECONOMIC INDEPENDENCE

B eneath Sudan's soil there lies vast reserves of gold, oil, copper, uranium and other valuable minerals. All these resources are historically underutilized or exploited by elites. Sudan's wealth has often been a course of conflict and economic stability.

If true economic independence is to be achieved, Sudan must break away from the vicious cycle of resource mismanagement and build a transparent mining sector that is well regulated. By harnessing its mineral resources effectively, Sudan can diversify its economy, attract investment, create jobs, and reduce dependency on foreign aid.

This chapter explores Sudan's vast mineral wealth, the challenges that have prevented its full utilization, and the strategic steps needed to turn Sudan into a global leader in sustainable resource extraction.

Sudan's Mineral Wealth: An Untapped Fortune

Sudan's mineral reserves are among the most valuable in Africa and worldwide. The country possesses:

1. Gold: Sudan's losing billions in revenue from illegal and informal gold smuggling.
2. Oil: Even though an important part of Sudan's oil reserve is lost.
3. Copper and Iron: These resources remain unexplored.
4. Uranium and Rare Earth Minerals: These resources have a critical role to play in tech and energy industries.
5. Marble, Manganese and Zinc: If appropriately developed and managed could contribute to industrialization and exports.

Sudan still remains economically fragile due to inflation, unemployment and weak currency.

The Challenges of Sudan's Mining Sector

Smuggling, poor regulation and continuous conflict led to Sudan's mineral wealth being squandered.

Barriers preventing Sudan from benefiting fully from resources:

1. Widespread Smuggling and Illegal Mining
2. Lack of Transparency
3. Poor Infrastructure and Outdated Technology
4. Environmental and Social Costs

For Sudan to fully benefit from its natural wealth, it must reform its mining sector, introduce sustainable practices, and ensure that mineral revenues benefit the nation as a whole.

A Blueprint for Sustainable Resource Development

A comprehensive national mining strategy must be implemented in order to transform Sudan into an economic hub. Six pillars of the transformation are below:

1. Establishing a Transparent and Accountable Resource Governance System
2. Formalizing and Regulating Artisanal Mining
3. Developing Local Processing and Value-Added Industries
4. Investing in Mining Infrastructure
5. Environmental and Social Responsibility
6. Attracting Ethical Foreign Investment

Sudan needs foreign expertise and investment, but on Sudan's terms. This means:
- Ensuring fair royalty agreements with international mining firms.
- Requiring technology transfer, so Sudanese workers gain mining expertise.
- Prioritizing deals that include local hiring and skills development.

Sudan must negotiate from a position of strength, ensuring foreign investments benefit the country rather than exploit its resources.

Sudan's Golden Opportunity

If Sudan reforms its mining sector, strengthens governance, and invests in processing industries, it can turn its mineral wealth into a long-term driver of economic independence.

- Gold revenues could stabilize Sudan's currency and fund development projects.
- Copper, uranium, and rare minerals could fuel Sudan's industrial growth.
- A modern mining industry could create thousands of jobs for Sudanese citizens.

The next chapter will explore Sudan's infrastructure needs and how strategic investment in roads, energy, and technology can lay the foundation for a modern economy. Sudan's minerals must be used to build; the time for a responsible resource revolution is now.

CHAPTER 8

INFRASTRUCTURE FOR TOMORROW: REBUILDING THE FOUNDATIONS OF SUDAN'S ECONOMY

No nation can achieve sustained economic growth without reliable infrastructure. Roads, bridges, railways, energy grids, and digital networks bridge the gap of a modern economy, allowing businesses to operate efficiently, farmers to bring their goods to market, and people to access essential services.

Without an infrastructure transformation, Sudan will struggle to compete in regional and global markets.

This chapter outlines the areas of infrastructure that Sudan needs to develop and present a clear strategy for rebuilding the nation's foundations to support economic revival and modernization.

The State of Sudan's Infrastructure: A Nation Left Behind

Infrastructure in Sudan is severely lacking across multiple sectors:

1. Roads and Transport
   - Less than 30% of Sudan's roads are paved, making transportation slow, expensive, and dangerous.
   - Many rural areas remain completely isolated, preventing farmers from reaching markets.
   - Poor roads increase the cost of goods, making food and essential items more expensive for ordinary Sudanese people.
2. Railways and Ports
   - Sudan once had a well-functioning railway system, but today, it is outdated and largely non-operational.
   - The country has a strategic coastline along the Red Sea, but its ports lack modern equipment and capacity, reducing trade efficiency.
3. Energy and Electricity
   - Frequent power outages; reliable electricity is rare with less than half of the population having access.
   - Full capacity operations are not possible due to unstable power supply.
   - Renewable energy potential (solar and hydro) remains untapped.
4. Water and Sanitation
   - Lack of access to clean drinking water, leading to waterborne diseases and health crises.
   - Poor sanitation has resulted in outbreaks of cholera.
5. Digital Connectivity and Telecommunications
   - Low internet penetration rates, limiting opportunities in technology and e-commerce.
   - Sudan's tech sector remains relatively modest.

If Sudan does not urgently modernize its infrastructure, it will remain trapped in economic stagnation and underdevelopment.

A Blueprint for Sudan's Infrastructure Development

A bold and ambitious infrastructure strategy must be implemented in order for Sudan to rebuild and modernize.

1. Revitalizing Roads, Railways, and Ports
   Transport system that functions well is essential for economic growth, trade, and investment.
   Sudan must prioritize the following actions:
   Roads
   - Expand major highways connecting Sudan's economic centres (Khartoum, Port Sudan, El Obeid, Nyala, Kassala).
   - Development of rural roads in order for farmers and businesses to transport goods efficiently.
   - Public-private partnerships (PPP) can help fund road expansion projects.
   Railways
   - Transform Sudan's railway network to reduce transportation costs and improve trade.
   - Modernize cargo rail systems to transport goods to ports and neighbouring countries.
   - Increase regional commerce by integrating Sudan's rail system with East African trade routes.
   Ports
   - Upgrade Port Sudan to improve capacity and efficiency in managing exports and imports.

- Develop secondary ports along the Red Sea to reduce congestion and attract international shipping companies.
- Introduce digital tracking systems to streamline logistics.

Investing in transport infrastructure will create jobs, reduce trade costs, and attract foreign investment.

2. Expanding Energy and Power Generation
   Sudan's economic development cannot happen without a reliable energy supply. The country must significantly expand and diversify its power generation by investing in:
   Hydropower
   - Expand hydroelectric dams and generate clean energy by utilizing Nile Water.
   - Upgrade existing dams to increase efficiency and reliability.
   Solar and Wind Energy
   - Even though Sudan has one of the highest solar energy potentials in Africa, it has not invested sufficiently in solar farms.
   - Develop large-scale solar energy projects to power cities and rural areas.
   - Wind farms in eastern Sudan could also provide sustainable energy solutions.
   Natural Gas and Oil Refining
   - Sudan still has significant oil reserves, but it must build refining capacity to reduce reliance on expensive fuel imports.
   - Investing in natural gas infrastructure can provide a cheaper and cleaner energy source.

By diversifying its energy sources, Sudan can reduce power shortages, lower electricity costs, and attract industries that require reliable energy.

3. Ensuring Water Security and Sanitation
    Access to clean water and sanitation is a basic human right and a key driver of health and economic productivity. Sudan must:
    –   Develop irrigation systems to increase agricultural production.
    –   Build modern water treatment facilities to ensure clean drinking water for everyone.
    –   Improve sanitation in cities and rural areas to reduce disease outbreaks.
    –   Introduce efficient water management policies to prevent overuse and pollution.

A modern water and sanitation system will reduce health risks, improve quality of life, and support economic activities.

4. Investing in Digital Connectivity and Telecommunications
    In the 21st century, digital infrastructure is just as important as roads and electricity. Sudan must:
    –   Expand internet access to rural and underserved areas.
    –   Develop high-speed fibre-optic networks to improve connectivity.
    –   Promote digital literacy programmes to prepare Sudan's workforce for modern jobs.
    –   Encourage tech startups and innovation hubs to grow Sudan's digital economy. E-commerce,

online education, and digital banking can
flourish if Sudan develops a strong digital
infrastructure.

5. Financing Infrastructure Development
   To fund these ambitious projects, Sudan must
   explore multiple financing options:

1. Public-Private Partnerships (PPP): Collaborate
   with international companies.
2. Foreign Direct Investment (FDI): Attract investors
   from Gulf countries, China, and the EU.
3. African Development Bank and World Bank
   Loans: Secure development loans for strategic
   infrastructure expansion.
4. Infrastructure Bonds: Issue government-backed
   bonds to raise domestic funding.

Sudan cannot rely solely on external aid it must develop
long-term financing models that ensure sustainability and
national ownership of key infrastructure projects.

The Future of Sudan's Infrastructure

Without concrete infrastructure, Sudan cannot compete in
the modern global economy.
   If Sudan prioritizes infrastructure investment, the
benefits will be great:

- Lower transportation costs, making Sudanese
  goods more competitive.
- Reliable electricity, attracting industries and
  foreign investors.

- Digital transformation, creating jobs and expanding the tech economy.
- Clean water and sanitation, improving health and productivity.

Infrastructure is the foundation of a strong economy. If Sudan commits to building for the future, it can become a regional leader in trade, agriculture, and industry.

The next chapter will explore Sudan's greatest assets, its people and how investing in education and healthcare will be essential to the nation's long-term success. Sudan's human capital will determine its future.

CHAPTER 9

EMPOWERING PEOPLE

Education and Healthcare as the Pillars of Sudan's Future

A nation's most valuable resource is not its land, minerals, or industries, it is the people. No country has ever achieved long term economic success without investing in education and healthcare. A well-educated, healthy population is the foundation of a concrete economy, a stable society, and an innovative future.

Yet, in Sudan, millions lack access to quality education and healthcare. Decades of underfunding and neglect have left schools in ruins, hospitals under-equipped, and essential services out of reach for large segments of the population. Without urgent reforms, Sudan will remain stuck in a cycle of poverty and underdevelopment.

This chapter explores Sudan's education and healthcare, their impact on national progress, and the urgent reforms needed to empower the Sudanese people.

The State of Education in Sudan: A System in Collapse

Sudan once had one of the strongest education systems in Africa, but today, it faces severe challenges:

- Three million plus children are out of school, especially in conflict-affected areas.
- Literacy rates are among the lowest in the region, with many people unable to read or write.
- Many schools lack basic facilities, such as electricity, clean water, and accredited teachers.
- Higher education and the job market have a huge gap in between, leaving graduates without employment opportunities.

Instead of preparing the next generation for leadership, Sudan's education system has become a barrier to progress.

How to Fix Sudan's Education System

To rebuild Sudan's education sector, a national education reform strategy must focus on five key priorities:

1. Access to Primary and Secondary Education
    Every Sudanese child must have access to quality education, regardless of their background or location. This requires:
    - Building and rehabilitating schools in rural and conflict-affected areas.
    - Providing free and compulsory primary education to ensure all children can attend school.
    - Training and hiring more teachers, offering competitive salaries to attract qualified professionals.
    - Investing in school feeding programmes to ensure children from poor families stay in school.

Sudan's future depends on educating its youth; without this, economic progress will be impossible.

2. Modernizing the Curriculum
    Sudan's education system is outdated, failing to prepare students for the modern economy. Reforms must include:
    –   STEM subjects inclusion (Science, Technology, Engineering, Mathematics) to build a workforce ready for the global market.
    –   Vocational training in industries such as agriculture, mining, and technology to create employment.
    –   Introducing digital tools in education to bring Sudanese students up to global standards.
        A modern curriculum will equip students with skills needed for Sudan's economic transformation.

3. Higher Education Reform and University Modernization
    Sudan's universities have thousands of graduates each year; however, many struggle to find jobs. To bridge this gap, Sudan must:
    –   Align university programmes with job market demands, ensuring students graduate with employable skills.
    –   Expand research and innovation centres, promoting scientific discovery and entrepreneurship.
    –   Encourage partnerships between universities and industries, ensuring graduates can transition into the workforce.

Sudanese universities must become engines of innovation and economic growth.

4. Expanding Adult Literacy and Lifelong Learning Programmes
   - Millions of Sudanese adults never had access to formal education. Sudan must invest in:
   - National literacy programmes to ensure every adult can read and write.
   - Technical and vocational training for workers, supporting their adaptation.
   - Online and distance learning initiatives, allowing access to education regardless of location.

Education should not end at childhood; lifelong learning is essential for national progress.

5. Financing Education Reform
   Education reform requires investment, but Sudan's government has historically underfunded this sector. To finance reforms, Sudan must:
   - Allocate a minimum of 20% of the budget to education.
   - Encourage public-private partnerships to fund new schools and universities.
   - Seek support from international donors and organizations, ensuring funding is used efficiently.

A strong education system is not an expense, but is an investment in Sudan's future.

The State of Healthcare in Sudan: A Crisis in Public Health

Sudan's healthcare system is one of the weakest in Africa, with millions of people unable to access basic medical services. Key issues include:

- Only 30% of Sudanese have access to proper healthcare, with rural areas suffering the most.
- Hospitals and clinics lack basic essential medicines, equipment, and trained staff.
- High maternal and infant mortality rates, with many women dying due to lack of prenatal care.
- Frequent outbreaks of preventable diseases, such as cholera and malaria.
- Shortage of doctors and nurses, as many leave Sudan for better opportunities abroad.

Without a functioning healthcare system, Sudan cannot improve living conditions or build a productive workforce.

How to Fix Sudan's Healthcare System

A comprehensive healthcare reform plan must be adopted by Sudan. It is a plan with four pillars:

1. Expanding Access to Healthcare Services
   Everyone must have access to affordable, quality healthcare. This requires:
   - Building up to date hospitals and clinics especially in rural and conflict-affected areas.
   - Expanding mobile health services, using technology to reach remote communities.

- Increasing the number of trained medical professionals, offering competitive salaries to retain talent.

Without universal healthcare access, Sudan will continue to suffer from high disease and mortality rates.

2. Investing in Preventative Healthcare
   Prevention is better and more effective than treatment. Sudan must:
   - Launch vaccination campaigns to prevent diseases.
   - Expand maternal and child health programmes, reducing mortality rates.
   - Promote clean water and sanitation initiatives, to prevent the spread of infections.

Investing in preventative care will reduce healthcare costs and improve overall public health.

3. Strengthening Healthcare Infrastructure and Technology
   Sudan's hospitals and clinics are outdated. To modernize healthcare, Sudan must:
   - Upgrade the medical facilities' equipment and supplies.
   - Develop a national health information system, to enable tracking of patient data.
   - Encourage digital healthcare solutions.

Modernizing Sudan's healthcare infrastructure will improve efficiency and save lives.

4. Ensuring Sustainable Healthcare Financing
   Healthcare reform requires long-term funding.
   Sudan can finance healthcare through:
   - Increasing government healthcare spending,
     ensuring hospitals have necessary resources.
   - Developing a national health insurance
     programme, giving citizens access to medical
     care.
   - Seeking investment ensures people receive
     high-quality care.

Healthcare should not be a luxury; it must be a right for everyone.

Empowering Sudan's People: The Key to Economic Transformation

Investing in education and healthcare is the most powerful tool for rebuilding Sudan. An educated and healthy nation will:
- Develop a skilled workforce, boosting investment and productivity.
- Reduction of inequality and poverty to improve the standard of living.
- Strengthen social stability, as educated, healthy populations are less prone to conflict.
- Ensuring long-term national development through increased life expectancy.

Sudan's future prosperity depends on how well it invests in its people today.

The next chapter will explore Sudan's role in the global economy, outlining how the country can attract foreign investment, strengthen regional trade, and integrate into global markets. Sudan must not only rebuild itself internally but also position itself as a key player on the world stage.

CHAPTER 10

GLOBAL PARTNERSHIPS: SUDAN'S ROLE IN THE REGIONAL AND GLOBAL ECONOMY

Sudan is strategically positioned with its vast natural resources, fertile lands, and access to the Red Sea; Sudan is stationed to become a key player in regional trade, international markets, and global investment networks.

Sudan is one of the under integrated economies in the world. Years of economic mismanagement, conflict, and sanctions have left Sudan isolated, unable to fully leverage its geographic and economic strengths.

Sudan must be reinstated in its place in the global economy. It must attract foreign investments, modernize key industries, strengthen regional trade alliances and position itself as the economic hub in Africa and beyond.

This chapter outlines Sudan's strategic opportunities in the global economy, the challenges it must overcome, and the steps needed to fully integrate into international markets.

Sudan's Strategic Economic Advantages

Three key advantages Sudan should benefit from:

1. Geographic Position as a Trade Hub
    Sudan's location between Africa, the Middle East,
    and the Red Sea gives it a natural advantage in
    trade and logistics.
    –   Sudan's Red Sea coastline provides access to
        international shipping routes.
    –   It shares borders with seven countries (Egypt,
        Libya, Chad, Central African Republic,
        South Sudan, Ethiopia, Eritrea), creating
        opportunities for regional trade corridors.
    –   Sudan can serve as a transit point for goods
        moving between Africa, the Gulf, and Asia.

If Sudan develops its ports, highways and railways, it can
become a major logistics hub, handling trade for landlocked
African nations and Gulf economies.

2. Natural Resource Wealth and Agricultural Potential
    –   Sudan has the potential to supply food,
        livestock, and raw materials to African, Middle
        Eastern, European, and Asian markets,
        giving it an opportunity to become the largest
        agricultural exporter in Africa.
    –   With optimum regulation and investment,
        Sudan's gold, oil, and mineral resources could
        be major revenue generators.
    –   Renewable energy investments (solar, hydro,
        and wind power) could position Sudan as an
        energy exporter to African and Gulf markets.

By focusing on sustainable development of its resources, Sudan can create long-term export industries that strengthen its economy.

3. A Young and Growing Workforce
   Sudan has a demographic advantage – over 60% of its population is under the age of 30.
   - Sudan must invest in education, vocational training, and technology.
   - Countries with young, skilled workforces often become industrial hubs.
   - Sudan's diaspora community includes many highly educated professionals who could return and contribute to the country's economic transformation.

A well-skilled, highly productive workforce will position Sudan as a global player in agriculture, mining, logistics, and technology.

Challenges to Sudan's Global Economic Integration

Sudan faces obstacles that must be addressed before it can fully integrate into the global economy.

1. Political Instability and Policy Uncertainty
   - Foreign investors are not interested in politically unstable environments.
   - Lack of clear economic policies alongside frequent government changes discourage investments.

- Sudan must establish political stability, ensure legal protections for investors, and create a predictable business environment.
2. Weak Infrastructure and Trade Barriers
    - Unstable road networks, outdated railways, and lack of efficient ports make trade expensive and slow.
    - Bureaucratic red tape creates barriers to business expansion.
    - Digital infrastructure limits Sudan's ability to participate in the global technology economy.
3. Limited Foreign Investment Due to Reputation and Sanctions History
    - Sudan's history of sanctions, human rights violations, and economic isolation has diminished its reputation among investors.
    - The country needs to rebuild trust with international financial institutions and demonstrate transparency through economic reform.

To succeed, Sudan must address these challenges head-on while positioning itself as a reliable economic partner.

Sudan's Economic Future: A Global Vision

Sudan is at a turning point. It can continue on the path of economic isolation and underdevelopment, or it can embrace global integration and modern economic reforms.

If this plan is followed, Sudan would be:

- A major agricultural exporter to Africa and the Gulf.

- A regional hub for mining and energy industries.
- A logistics and trade centre connecting Africa to the world.
- A leader in digital transformation and innovation.

The next chapter will explore how Sudan can ensure good governance and transparency, laying the institutional foundations necessary for long-term economic success. Sudan must not only develop its economy but also ensure it is managed wisely for the benefit of everyone.

CHAPTER 11

GOOD GOVERNANCE: FIGHTING CORRUPTION AND BUILDING INSTITUTIONS FOR SUDAN'S FUTURE

Sustainable development cannot be achieved without strong institutions, transparency in governance and functioning legal systems. Sudan's history is marked by authoritarian rule, which has systematically weakened its economy, eroded public trust, and hindered foreign investment.

If Sudan is to rebuild and establish itself as a stable, prosperous nation, good governance must be the foundation of its transformation.

Without accountability, even the best economic policies will fail. A strong judicial system, democratic institutions, and effective public administration are essential for Sudan to break free from its past and build a new future.

This chapter examines the impact of poor governance in Sudan, the urgent need for reform, and the practical steps required to build a government that serves its people rather than exploits them.

Good governance must be the pillar of Sudan's transformation in order for Sudan to rebuild itself.

The Importance of Rural Development in Sudan

Rural development is a very important factor in Sudan's progress. Nearly 65% of the population of Sudan resides in rural areas; the country's prosperity is heavily dependent on improving rural infrastructure, agriculture, and basic services. Investing in rural development can lead to food security and poverty reduction. Exploration of the significance of rural development in Sudan and investment in economic stability and social progress is crucial.

1. Economic Stability and Agricultural Productivity

The economy of Sudan is heavily dependent on agriculture, which is a large part of the country's GDP. The fact is, that in rural areas, the levels of suffering from poor infrastructure and outdated farming, limits both productivity and the economic success of the country. Investment in modern irrigation systems, improved seeds, and training programmes for farmers can significantly enhance yields, reduce post-harvest losses, and increase income for rural communities.

The support of small-scale farmers through financial aid, and access to technology can boost the economy. This would not only create jobs but also add value to agricultural products before they reach urban markets or international exports. Enhancing road networks and storage facilities would further facilitate efficient transportation and minimize losses, ensuring that rural communities benefit from a more robust agricultural supply chain.

The potential to expand Sudan's agro-industry is great. There needs to be rural-based processing industries.

2. Poverty Reduction and Employment Generation

One of the biggest challenges Sudan faces is rural poverty. Communities filled with lack of access to basic necessities, clean water, healthcare, education and electricity. Rural development programmes can bring essential services and create employment. By promoting diversified income-generating activities: livestock farming, beekeeping, and handicrafts, rural families can be financially independent. Additionally, microfinance initiatives can help rural entrepreneurs establish small businesses. When rural economies are strengthened, they become more self-sufficient and resilient to economic shocks, including climate-related challenges and political instability.

3. Food Security and Climate Resilience

Food insecurity due to floods, droughts, and conflict that interfere with agricultural production is a major challenge in Sudan.

Rural development investment is highly required via climate smart agricultural practices, reforestation programmes and conservation techniques. These channels can enhance resilience against challenges from the environment. Additionally, investment in irrigation systems and improved land management will help navigate the effects of climate change on food production.

Moreover, promoting community-based agricultural cooperatives and supporting research institutions in developing sustainable farming methods will contribute to long-term food security. Strengthening rural food systems ensures access to affordable and nutritious food, reducing dependence on food aid and imports.

4. Social Stability and National Cohesion

Neglecting rural areas has proven to contribute to the impact on social and political unrest in Sudan. Disparities between urban and rural development lead to grievances. By prioritizing rural development, the government promotes inclusive growth and reduces tensions that arise from economic injustices.

Improving education and healthcare in rural areas is essential in creating social stability. Investing in schools, vocational training centres, and medical facilities ensures that rural populations have opportunities for personal and professional growth. When people feel included in national development efforts, they are more likely to contribute positively to society and support peacebuilding initiatives.

Rural development is not only an economic necessity but also a fundamental pillar of Sudan's long-term stability and prosperity. Strengthening agricultural productivity, reducing poverty, ensuring food security, and fostering social cohesion are the main benefits of investing in rural communities. The government, private sector, and international organizations must work together to create and implement programmes and policies that empower rural populations, creating a more balanced and sustainable future for Sudan. Sudan can unlock full potential and make meaningful progress for all its people.

Civil Service Reform in Sudan: Challenges and Prospects

Due to the country's complex political history, economic challenges and institutional inefficiencies, civil service reform in Sudan is an urgent issue. The civil service has suffered from inefficiency, overstaffing, corruption and lack of a good recruitment screening process. The civil service has important functions in service delivery, national development and governance. The need for reform has become even more urgent in the wake of Sudan's political transitions, economic hardships, and efforts to integrate into the global economy.

Historical Context

It was the British colonial administration that had originally modelled the Sudanese civil service system. They established a framework that was bureaucratic and effectively ran for decades. However, post-independence governments politicized the civil service, leading to a decline in its effectiveness. After the 2019 revolution there were renewed efforts to reform the civil service, but these efforts were challenged by political instability and economic crises.

Key Challenges in Civil Service Reform

1. Politicization and Lack of Meritocracy
    Sudan's deep-rooted politicization is one of the biggest obstacles to achieving civil service reform.

For years, appointments were not based on competency but rather on political loyalty. This practice has led to inefficiency, corruption, and a lack of accountability.

2. Overstaffing and Bureaucratic Inefficiency
    The civil service is overstaffed with employees who lack proper qualifications, training and clear roles. This led to inefficiency and low productivity.

3. Corruption and Lack of Transparency
    Civil service's performance is affected by corruption. Misuse of public funding and nepotism have been very frequent. Reform must include transparency, strong anti-corruption measures and accountability.

4. Outdated Administrative Structures and Technology
    The administrative structure that the civil service operates is outdated, not digitized. The offices lack modern management systems; this leads to inefficiency and delays.

5. Weak Policy Implementation and Legal Frameworks
    Even though other governments have introduced reform plans, implementation has often been lacking due to political interference, resistance from entrenched interests, and lack of technical capacity.

To ensure enforcement mechanisms are in place, the legal frameworks must be strengthened.

Strategies for Effective Reform

1. Depoliticization and Merit-Based Recruitment
    Political interference in the hiring process must be
    eliminated. A merit-based recruitment system is
    essential. Civil servants should be hired based on
    qualifications, experience, and performance rather
    than political affiliations.

2. Rightsizing the Workforce and Capacity Building
    A comprehensive audit must be conducted to
    identify redundant positions and streamline the
    workforce. Investments in training and professional
    development are necessary to improve the skills of
    public sector employees.

3. Combating Corruption and Enhancing
    Transparency
    Digitalization of government services, such as
    online procurement and financial management
    systems, can help combat corruption.

    Promoting a culture of accountability and
    implementing strict anti-corruption laws is crucial.

4. Modernizing Administrative Processes
    A transition to e-governance can significantly
    improve efficiency, reduce paperwork, and enhance
    service. Implementing automated systems for
    payroll, human resources, and public services
    will create a more transparent and responsive
    bureaucracy.

5. Strengthening Institutional and Legal Frameworks

Legal and regulatory reforms are required to provide a solid foundation for a professional and independent civil service. Establishing clear laws governing performance evaluation, recruitment, promotions, and disciplinary measures will help ensure accountability.

Civil service reform in Sudan is an urgent necessity for building a capable, transparent, and efficient government that can serve the needs of the people. While past efforts have been undermined by political instability, a well-structured and sustained reform strategy can lead to significant improvements. By depoliticizing the civil service, investing in human capital, embracing digital transformation, and enforcing anti-corruption measures, Sudan can create a public administration system that fosters economic growth, stability, and good governance.

The Impact of Poor Governance on Sudan's Development

For decades, Sudan has suffered from political instability and weak institutions, leading to:

1. Loss of Public Trust
   - People view the government as self-serving.
   - People often rely on informal networks or tribal connections rather than the state to resolve disputes and access services.
2. Economic Mismanagement and Corruption
   - Billions in gold, oil, and tax revenues have been lost.

- State-owned enterprises have been misused rather than used as engines of economic growth.
3. Weak Rule of Law and Human Rights Violations
   - The lack of a strong judiciary and rule of law caused politically motivated arrests.
   - Ethnic discrimination has motivated conflicts and broken national unity.
4. Barriers to Investment and Growth
   - Foreign investors avoid Sudan due to legal uncertainties.
   - Business regulations are unclear, making it difficult for companies to operate.

Unless Sudan has a strong, accountable governance, it will remain trapped in cycles of economic failure.

The Foundations of Good Governance

For Sudan to establish a democratic, transparent, and effective government, reforms must focus on four key pillars:

1. Strengthening Institutions and the Rule of Law
2. Ensuring Transparent Public Finance Management
3. Building Inclusive and Representative Leadership
4. Empowering Civil Society and Free Press

1. Strengthening Institutions and the Rule of Law
   A functioning state requires independent political interference and strong institutions. Sudan must:
   - Ensure judges are independent.
   - Train law agencies to uphold human rights and practise the law fairly.

- Ensure free and fair elections that reflect the will of the people.
- Decentralize government power, giving authority to local administrations rather than concentrating it in Khartoum.

A government that respects the rule of law will gain legitimacy and create a stable environment for investment and development. In this respect enforcement agencies must be straightened.

2. Ensuring Transparent Public Finance Management

One of Sudan's biggest governance failures has been financial mismanagement. Government funds have often been lost, or misused, depriving people of essential services. To fix this, Sudan must:

- Publish national budgets and government spending reports so the public can see where money is going.
- Independent audits of all state agencies and major projects to be introduced.
- Sovereign Wealth Fund is to be created in order to manage resource revenues transparently, ensuring oil and gold profits benefit the public.
- Implement digital tax collection to prevent corruption and ensure revenue reaches the government.

3. Building Inclusive and Representative Leadership

To build a truly representative democracy, Sudan must:

- Ensure fair representation of all ethnic and regional groups in government institutions.
- Strengthen women's participation in politics, ensuring gender equality in leadership roles.

- Encourage youth engagement in governance, bringing fresh ideas and reducing the influence of old power structures.
- Ensuring civilians can have some control over national security.

4. Empowering Civil Society and Free Press
   A thriving democracy requires a strong civil society and an independent media that holds the government accountable. Sudan must:
   - Ensure press freedom, allowing journalists to report without fear of government repression.
   - Support independent NGOs and civic groups, giving citizens a voice in policy decisions.
   - Introduce freedom of information laws, ensure government documents accessible to the public.
   - Encourage public participation in governance, using digital platforms to engage citizens in decision-making.

A government that fears its own people cannot be trusted. Sudan must embrace transparency, public engagement, and media freedom.

The Path to a Stable, Prosperous Sudan

Sudan has suffered too long under weak institutions. But change is possible. Countries like Ghana, Rwanda, and Botswana have successfully reformed their governance structures, resulting in economic growth, political stability, and international credibility.

If Sudan adopts strong governance reforms, the benefits will be enormous:

- Increased public trust, as citizens see their government working for them.
  - Higher foreign investment, as global businesses gain confidence in Sudan's stability.
  - Economic growth, as corruption is reduced and resources are allocated efficiently.
  - Stronger national unity, as all Sudanese feel represented in government.
  - Greater international recognition, allowing Sudan to play a stronger role in global affairs.

Good governance is not a luxury, it is a necessity for Sudan's survival and future prosperity. Without transparency, accountability, and strong institutions, Sudan will remain stuck in the past.

Sudan's Stolen Heritage:

A Crisis Demanding Urgent Action

The war in Sudan has created a devastating humanitarian and cultural catastrophe. Among the most egregious consequences has been the widespread looting and smuggling of the nation's museums by the Rapid Support Forces (RSF), allied militias, and opportunistic criminal networks. These actors have plundered irreplaceable treasures that reflect thousands of years of Sudanese history – artefacts from the ancient Kingdom of Kush, Nubian civilizations, Islamic heritage, and colonial-era archives. These cultural assets are not merely museum pieces; they are priceless testaments to Sudan's identity, dignity, and its rightful place in the story of global civilization.

The illegal trafficking of these artefacts across Sudan's porous borders into neighbouring countries represents both a loss of heritage and a blow to national pride. This cultural theft, often overshadowed by military and humanitarian dimensions of the conflict, must be treated with the same level of urgency. Restoring Sudan's looted heritage is not only a moral and legal imperative, it is essential to national healing, cultural continuity, and post-war reconstruction.

Measures to Restore Sudan's Cultural Wealth

1. **International Coordination and Legal Action**: The Sudanese government, alongside cultural institutions and international organizations such as UNESCO, INTERPOL, and the World Customs Organization, must coordinate to identify, track, and repatriate stolen treasures and artefacts. This includes launching a formal international appeal for assistance, placing looted items on international watchlists, and enforcing strict import/export controls through legal and diplomatic pressure on neighbouring states.

2. **Digital Cataloguing and Verification**: Before the war, many Sudanese museums maintained limited or non-digitized records. A robust, digitized inventory of stolen items is critical. Collaborating with international universities, museums, and tech partners, a comprehensive digital catalogue should be created – detailing photographs, provenance, and historical context of each piece. This database will serve as a reference for border agencies, auction houses, collectors, and law enforcement worldwide.

3. **Border Monitoring and Anti-Smuggling Measures**: Sudan's borders must be a focus for regional security cooperation. Joint security task forces involving Sudan's neighbours – such as Egypt, Ethiopia, Chad, and South Sudan – should be established to crack down on the

smuggling routes used to traffic artefacts. Satellite imagery, drone surveillance, and coordinated ground patrols can significantly aid these efforts.

4. **Sanctions and Accountability**: The RSF and affiliated militias must be held accountable for cultural crimes under international law. The looting of cultural property during armed conflict is a violation of the 1954 Hague Convention and other legal instruments. Sanctions should be imposed on individuals, entities, and networks found complicit in trafficking, and mechanisms must be set in place to seize and return artefacts from foreign museums, private collections, or black-market dealers.

5. **Public Awareness and Advocacy**: A strong global advocacy campaign – engaging the media, academic institutions, and the Sudanese diaspora – can elevate the urgency of heritage recovery. Awareness efforts will pressure foreign governments and institutions to cooperate, and may also encourage individuals in possession of looted items to return them voluntarily.

6. **Post-Conflict Museum Reconstruction**: Long-term efforts must focus on rebuilding and securing Sudan's museums and cultural institutions. This includes restoring physical infrastructure, training staff in preservation and security, and creating public programmes to reconnect Sudanese citizens – especially the youth – with their cultural legacy. The protection of heritage should be integrated into national recovery and reconciliation strategies.

The restoration of Sudan's cultural heritage is not merely about retrieving stolen treasures and artefacts; it is about reclaiming history, restoring identity, and reinforcing the values of justice and sovereignty. As the world watches Sudan endure the turmoil of war, it must also act to preserve and return the soul of a nation – its heritage.

The next chapter will focus on Sudan's greatest assets, its women and youth, and how empowering them will drive national transformation. Sudan's young, dynamic population holds the key to a new era of innovation, economic success, and social progress.

CHAPTER 12

THE ROLE OF WOMEN AND THE YOUTH IN REBUILDING SUDAN

Without the empowerment of women and the youth no nation can achieve long lasting progress. Sudan is a population of young people and resilient women. They represent the greatest untapped resource for the transformation of Sudan. However, for years both have been underrepresented.

The Revolution of December 2019 demonstrated the power of Sudan's youth and women who were at the forefront of the movements that led to the ousting of Omar al-Bashir. Despite demanding justice and democracy, they still face systemic barriers in political, social and economic aspects.

This chapter examines the challenges faced by youths and women. The impact of exclusion, and urgent reforms needed to empower them as leaders of Sudan's future.

The Challenges Facing Women and the Youth in Sudan

1. Political Exclusion
    –   Women and Youths have been underrepresented in government and decision-making bodies.

- Traditional structures favour older men making it difficult for young leaders and women.
- Gender-based discrimination norms prevent women from rising.

2. Economic Marginalization
   - Unemployment is one of the highest in Africa, leaving millions without income or career prospects.
   - Women face barriers when entering the workforce.
   - Most of the Sudanese youth and women turn to informal jobs with low wages and little security.

3. Limited Access to Education and Skills Training
   - Millions of young people are denied education.
   - Lack of preparation for youths for the job market. Leaving them without the skills needed for modern industries.
   - Technical and vocational training opportunities are scarce, preventing young people from gaining hands-on skills.

4. Legal and Social Barriers
   - Domestic violence and gender discrimination.
   - Child marriage.
   - Lack of social and political influence from youth.
   - Lack of representation in the legal system and does not fully protect women's rights or youth participation.

If Sudan does not urgently address these challenges, it will waste the talents, energy, and creativity of millions of people who could drive national progress.

The Impact of Excluding Women and Youths

When women and youths are excluded from economic and political life, the entire country suffers:
- Economic stagnation: Workforce remains underutilized, slowing productivity and innovation.
- Political instability: Youths without jobs or opportunities become frustrated increasing the risk of protests, crime, and radicalization.
- Missed opportunities for development: Many talented youths and women leave in search of better opportunities abroad.
- Weaker democracy: Without youths and women's participation, democracy remains incomplete and disconnected from the majority of the population.

Countries that prioritize gender equality and youth empowerment experience higher economic growth, lower poverty rates, and stronger governance. Sudan must fully integrate women and youths into its reconstruction efforts if it wants to succeed.

A Roadmap for Empowering Women and Youths

Women and youths must be at the centre of Sudan's rebuilding process, Sudan must implement urgent reforms in four key areas:

1. Political Empowerment and Leadership Inclusion Sudan must guarantee political representation for women and the youth by:

- Women must hold at least 40% leadership positions.
- Gender quotas in government and parliament should be implemented.
- Allowing young leaders to run for office by lowering the age for political candidacy.
- Inclusion of the youth and women in political party structures.
- Encouraging civic engagement programmes, training young people in leadership, governance, and policymaking.

When the youth and women hold power, they bring fresh ideas and commitment to national progress.

2. Economic Empowerment and Job Creation
   To integrate women and youths into Sudan's economy, the government must:
   - Implement more youth entrepreneurship programmes.
   - Business skills training.
   - Allowing women and young entrepreneurs to start and grow businesses by providing microfinance and business loans.
   - Create incentives for companies to hire young workers, offering tax benefits for businesses that employ the youth.
   - Develop apprenticeship programmes and make sure young people gain hands-on experience in agriculture, technology, manufacturing, and other key industries.

If Sudan's youth and women are given economic opportunities, they can drive the country's economic recovery.

3. Education and Skills Development for the Future
Sudan must reform its educational system and
prepare young people and women for the workforce
by:
   – Universal access to primary and secondary
     education, especially for girls in rural areas.
   – Upgrading school curriculums, modernization
     and development of technology, business, and
     practical skills.
   – Expanding vocational training centres,
     providing hands-on experience in high-demand
     fields.
   – Encouraging scholarships for women in STEM,
     giving them the opportunity to enter male-
     dominated industries.

An educated population creates innovation, attracts
investment, and strengthens national development.

4. Legal and Social Reforms to Protect Women and
the Youth
To remove legal and cultural barriers, Sudan must:
   – Make stronger laws that protect women's
     rights.
   – Criminalize gender-based violence.
   – Outlaw child marriage and forced marriage.
   – Ensure equal pay and protections for women.
   – Create youth engagement councils, giving
     young people a formal role in policymaking.
     Legal and social reforms will empower women
     and youths to take control of their futures.

The Power of Women and the Youth in Sudan's Future

If Sudan fully empowers its women and youths, it will observe:

- Exponential economic growth. Many skilled workers contribute to productivity.
- Stability in society. Lower rates of crime, radicalization, and political unrest.
- Global competitiveness as Sudan builds an innovative, knowledge-based economy.
- A more inclusive democracy, with fresh leadership and diverse representation.

Rwanda, Ethiopia, and Tunisia have successfully integrated women and youths into governance and the economy, which resulted in higher economic growth and improved national stability. If Sudan follows this example, it will bring inclusive leadership and development.

A Generation That Will Rebuild Sudan

The youth of Sudan and its women led the revolution that fought for democracy and change. Now, they must lead the next revolution, the one of economic growth, innovation, and national unity.

Sudan's future does not only belong to the past generations. Additionally, it belongs to the young men and women who have the courage, vision, and energy to transform their nation.

The next chapter will explore the role of Sudan in Africa and the world, focusing on how Sudan could become a leader in trade, diplomacy, and cultural influence. Sudan must not only rebuild itself but also strengthen its position as a key player on the African and global stage.

CHAPTER 13

GLOBAL PARTNERSHIPS: SUDAN'S PLACE IN AFRICA AND THE WORLD

Sudan stands at a political, economical and geographical crossroad. Sudan is positioned as a bridge between North Africa, Sub-Saharan Africa, and the Middle East.

For a long time, Sudan has been isolated from international trade, diplomacy and held back by political instability, internal conflicts, and sanctions.

As Sudan embarks on this new path of economic recovery and national revival, it should also redefine the role it has in Africa and the world. It's not possible to thrive in isolation. Sudan needs to actively engage in cooperation, global trade and diplomacy.

This chapter explores Sudan's strategic opportunities in Africa and beyond. The challenges it must overcome, and the policies needed to reintegrate Sudan into the global economy and international relations.

Sudan's Strategic Position as a Regional Power

Sudan's geographic and economic potential gives it three major advantages:

1. A Gateway Between Africa and the Middle East
   - Sudan has mutual historical, cultural, and economic ties with the Gulf states, including Saudi Arabia, the UAE, and Qatar.
   - Provides direct access to key global shipping routes through its coastline along the red sea.
   - Sudan can position itself as a trade hub.
2. A Critical Trade Partner in Africa
   - Sudan shares borders with seven African nations.
   - By strengthening transport infrastructure, Sudan can become a key supplier of agricultural goods, livestock, and minerals to the world.
   - Sudan's membership in the African Continental Free Trade Area (AfCFTA) allows access to an opportunity of a $3.4 trillion market.
3. Untapped Economic Potential in International Trade
   - Sudan has gold, oil, cotton, and livestock that could be leveraged for export.
   - Sudan can attract foreign direct investment (FDI) and develop an industrial base to compete in global markets.

To capitalize on these advantages, Sudan must work on its international partnerships, strengthen trade policies, and position itself as a reliable economic partner.

Challenges to Sudan's Global Integration

Despite its potential, Sudan faces significant obstacles in its quest for global reintegration:

1. Political and Economic Instability
   - Foreign investors are not confident enough to invest in Sudan due to political uncertainty and weak institutions.
   - The country's frequent economic fluctuations make it challenging to establish long-term trade agreements.
   - Sudan must establish its governance and legal framework to regain the trust of its people and global community.
2. Weak Infrastructure and Limited Connectivity
   - Sudan lacks upgraded and modern transport.
   - Poor roads, outdated railways, and limited port facilities make it more expensive to do business in Sudan.
   - Investment in infrastructure is a must in a competitive global trade partner.
3. The Legacy of Sanctions and Diplomatic Isolation
   - Economic sanctions and international isolation limit the ability to engage in global trade and diplomacy.
   - Needs restoration of its reputation, to rebuild relationships, and to attract foreign investment. By this I mean that the corporate image of the country itself must be improved.

Sudan must actively pursue regional and global economic integration through strong diplomatic and trade policies.

A Roadmap for Sudan's Global Engagement

Sudan must implement a strategic approach to international partnerships, trade, and diplomacy.

1. Strengthening Regional Trade and Economic Cooperation
2. Attracting Foreign Investment and Business Partnerships
3. Developing Sudan's Export Market and Industrial Base
4. Rebuilding Sudan's Diplomatic and International Relations
5. Investing in Technology and Digital Transformation

The Future of Sudan in the Global Economy

If Sudan plans and undertakes these strategic reforms, it has the potential to become:

- Top agri and food supplier to Africa and the world.
- A trade hub connecting African and Middle Eastern economies.
- A manufacturing and industrial centre, producing value-added goods for global markets.
- A top destination for foreign investment and business expansion.
- A leader in Diplomacy in Africa and beyond.

Sudan's success in the global economy will not come from isolation or reliance on raw material exports; it must actively build trade partnerships, attract investment, and modernize its industries.

The next chapter will dive into lessons from other countries that have successfully rebuilt after conflict and economic collapse. Key insights taken from other countries can be applied in Sudan's journey toward transformation. The nation must learn from history to forge a better future.

CHAPTER 14

LEARNING FROM THE WORLD LESSONS FROM NATIONS THAT REBUILT AFTER CONFLICT

History has demonstrated that even nations that have gone through war, economic collapse, and political turmoil can once again rise from the ashes. These countries rebuild into stable, prosperous societies. From post-war Germany and Japan to modern success stories like Rwanda and South Korea, there are valuable lessons Sudan can learn from countries that have overcome adversity.

Sudan's challenges – political instability, economic mismanagement and ethnic divisions – are similar to many other countries which successfully rebuilt by adopting strategic policies, investing in infrastructure, and prioritizing national unity.

This chapter examines key lessons from countries that have transformed after conflict and outlines how Sudan can apply these lessons to build a strong, resilient, and prosperous future.

Lesson 1: Germany and Japan: The Power of Economic Reconstruction

What Happened?

Germany and Japan were both left in ruins after World War II. The cities were completely destroyed, economies collapsed, and millions of people faced poverty. However, within two decades, they transformed into two of the strongest economies in the world.

How Did They Rebuild?

- Major investment in infrastructure and industry.
- Prioritization of education and technological development.
- Strong government-business cooperation.
- Creating stable policies that encouraged investment.
- Trade-focused economic policies.

Lesson for Sudan
Sudan must:
- Invest in infrastructure, roads, and energy to support growth.
- Develop a long-term industrial policy, focusing on value-added industries.
- Encourage foreign direct investment (FDI) by ensuring political and economic stability.
- Leverage international partnerships to rebuild and modernize its economy.

For Germany and Japan economic stability was put before politics – Sudan must do the same.

Lesson 2: Rwanda: Overcoming Division and Focusing on Development

What Happened?

Rwanda experienced one of the worst genocides in history (1994). Millions of people were killed in just 100 days. The economy collapsed, institutions failed, and ethnic divisions ran deep.

How Did Rwanda Rebuild?

- By utilising national reconciliation and creating unity programmes, all ethnic groups were represented in government.
- Instilled a Zero tolerance policy for corruption, making Rwanda one of the least corrupt countries in Africa.
- Strong investment in infrastructure, agriculture, and digital technology.
- Strategic regional and global trade partnerships, making Rwanda a hub for African business.

Lesson for Sudan
Sudan must:
- Prioritize national unity and reconciliation.
- Implement strict anti-corruption policies.
- Ensure public funds serve the people.
- Invest in agriculture, industry, and digital transformation.
- Develop regional trade partnerships, positioning Sudan as an economic hub in Africa.

Rwanda turned tragedy into opportunity through inclusive governance and economic reforms – Sudan must follow this model.

Lesson 3: South Korea: Investing in Human Capital and Innovation

What Happened?

Post-Korean War (1950-1953) South Korea became one of the poorest nations in the world. The infrastructure was destroyed, industries were weak, and it had little natural wealth. However, in just three decades, it became one of the world's leading economies.

How Did South Korea Rebuild?

- Major investment in education.
- Governmental support for industrial development.
- Export-driven economic policies.
- Strong anti-corruption measures.

Lesson for Sudan
Sudan must:
- Reform its education system.
- Encourage private-sector growth.
- Promote an export-driven economy.
- Invest in innovation and digital transformation.

Sudan must follow this model to build a strong, knowledge-based economy.

Lesson 4: Singapore: From Poverty to Global Economic Hub

What Happened?

Singapore(1960s) was a small, poor island with little natural resources and so much unemployment. Today, it is one of the richest and most competitive economies in the world.

How Did Singapore Rebuild?

- Strict anti-corruption laws.
- Massive infrastructure development.
- Investment in education and technology.
- Pro-business policies.

Lesson for Sudan
Sudan must:
- Fight corruption aggressively.
- Develop Port Sudan into a major trade hub, leveraging its strategic location on the Red Sea.
- Create an investment-friendly environment, attracting businesses to build industries in Sudan.
- Invest in digital technology and e-commerce, modernizing its economy.

Singapore proved that small countries with no resources can become global leaders through strategic economic planning and governance. Sudan must apply the same principles.

How Sudan Can Apply These Lessons

Sudan has all the raw materials for success – a young population, fertile land, rich resources, and a strategic location. However, it must learn from history and apply the right practices to achieve transformation.

Key Actions Sudan Must Take
- End political instability, promote democracy, and fight corruption.
- Develop modern industries, roads, ports, and energy systems.
- Prioritize technical training, STEM education, and digital transformation.
- Strengthen African trade ties and attract foreign investment.
- Invest in digital infrastructure and entrepreneurship to create new industries.

By applying these strategies, Sudan can rebuild its economy, strengthen its democracy, and secure a prosperous future.

The Road Ahead for Sudan

The examples of Germany, Japan, Rwanda, South Korea, and Singapore prove that any country, no matter how devastated, can once again rise with the optimum leadership, policies, and vision.

Sudan must now choose its path:
- Will it remain stuck in cycles of instability and poverty?

- Or will it take bold steps to rebuild, modernize, and become a leader in Africa?

The next chapter will explore how Sudan can achieve a long-term national development plan. A Marshall Plan for Sudan, that outlines a clear vision for economic recovery, social transformation, and global leadership.

CHAPTER 15

A CALL TO ACTION: BUILDING A RESURGENT SUDAN TOGETHER

For decades, Sudan has suffered political instability and war. Sudanese people have been through hardship, broken promises, and displacement.

Even though Sudan has been through so much, it never lost its spirit, resilience, and potential. Now, the country has a choice: continue on the path of instability, or rise to rebuild a nation that is strong, united, and prosperous.

This book has outlined a clear vision for Sudan's economic recovery, governance reforms, infrastructure modernization, human development, and global reintegration. But a vision is only as powerful as the actions taken to bring it to life. Sudan cannot wait for foreign solutions or short term fixes. It must take charge of its own destiny and commit to a long-term transformation.

This final chapter is a call to action for every leader, citizen, and international partner. The time for waiting is over. The future of Sudan must begin now.

A Nation's Transformation Starts with Leadership

No country in history has risen from crisis without strong, visionary leadership. Sudan's future will be determined by the decisions made today by its leaders.

1. Political Leaders: The Responsibility to Govern Justly
   Sudan's politicians must let go of their personal interests, ethnic divisions, and power struggles. To work towards building a stable future, they must:
   - Commit to democratic governance, and ensure fair elections and civilian rule.
   - End corruption, holding the government accountable to the people.
   - Prioritize unity over political power, building a Sudan for all.
   - Engage in long-term planning, rather than short-term policies that serve political survival. History will remember those who chose to build instead of destroy. Sudan's leaders must make the right choice.

2. Business Leaders: The Role of the Private Sector in Economic Growth
   Sudan cannot develop if its economy is dominated and state controlled. It is also an outdated industry. Private businesses and entrepreneurs must:
   - Expand manufacturing, agriculture, and technology.
   - Ensure economic inclusion.
   - Embrace innovation and digital transformation.
   - Demand government transparency and accountability.

- The private sector must become the engine of Sudan's transformation, driving sustainable economic growth.
3. Civil Society: The Power of the People
Real change does not come only from the top, it is built by the will and actions of the people.
Sudanese citizens must:
Hold their leaders accountable.
   - Demand transparency and reforms.
   - Participate in rebuilding efforts.
   - Promote peace and national unity.
   - Reject tribal and political divisions.
   - Support local businesses and industries
   - Build a self-sustaining economy.

Sudan belongs to all its people, and its future will be shaped by their collective actions.

Key Priorities for Sudan's Future

The transformation of Sudan will not happen in one day, but progress must begin immediately.

The following are the five urgent priorities Sudan must focus on in the coming decade:

1. Establish Political Stability and Governance Reform.
2. Rebuild the Economy and Infrastructure
3. Invest in Education, Healthcare, and Human Development
4. Strengthen Regional and Global Partnerships
5. Ensure Sustainable Development and Climate Resilience

These five pillars are not separate, they are interconnected and must be pursued together to create a strong, self-sufficient Sudan.

The Red Sea Treasures Between Sudan and Saudi Arabia

A Strategic Asset for Economic and Developmental Growth

The Red Sea is a critical maritime linkage between Africa and the Middle East. It harbours copious amounts of wealth beneath the waters.

Between Saudi Arabia and Sudan, there's a treasure which is not just limited to rich seabeds, oil and gas reserves. It is a marine ecosystem with environmental, geopolitical and economic significance.

The potential to reshape the economic landscapes of both Saudi Arabia and Sudan heavily rely on the resources, now more than ever, as Sudan forges a path of economic recovery. One of the landmark agreements governing the exploitation of these resources is the 1974 Agreement between Sudan and Saudi Arabia. This laid the foundation for joint exploration and equitable distribution of benefits. Understanding their economic potential, the significance of these treasures and their role in Sudan's reconstruction efforts is crucial in evaluating their long-term impact.

The Red Sea Treasures Between Sudan and Saudi Arabia: What They Are and What Do They Do?

The Red Sea holds a variety of natural treasures that have immense economic value, including:

1. Mineral Deposits and Hydrocarbons
   There exist extensive deposits of precious minerals beneath the seabed of the Red Sea. Such as gold, silver, copper, zinc, and cobalt, particularly in the Atlantis II Deep, a mineral-rich zone located in the central Red Sea between Sudan and Saudi Arabia. According to studies, it's been indicated that this area contains millions of tons of polymetallic sulphides. This makes it one of the world's most significant undersea mining sites. In addition to this, the oil and natural gas reserves in the Sudanese and Saudi maritime zones has piqued interest in offshore drilling that offers opportunities for economic expansion.

2. Fisheries and Marine Biodiversity
   The Red Sea supports so much marine life. Fisheries are one of the most valuable renewable resources. The deep sea ecosystems provide a sustainable source of trade and food. This benefits the coastal communities in both countries.

3. Tourism and Environmental Wealth
   Employment and foreign direct investment can be generated via growing interest and sustainable development in eco-tourism, diving and marine conservation. The 1974 Agreement Between Sudan and Saudi Arabia was aimed at regulation and exploitation of underwater wealth. The agreement established:
   – A framework for resources that are equitable.
   – Mining and oil exploration through the creation of joint ventures and partnerships.

- The allocation of research and development resources for undersea exploration.
- Legal mechanisms for dispute resolution and environmental sustainability.

The agreement laid the groundwork for collaborative projects including the Atlantis II mining mission. Even though there were many political and technological challenges over the years, the agreement still has a large importance over maritime cooperation between the two nations.

The Vast Economic Value of the Red Sea Treasures

The Red Sea has many resources that have so much economic potential and can change both the Sudanese and Saudi economies.

1. Boosting National Revenues
   Undersea minerals resources could generate billions of dollars annually. Sudan's economy needs diversification, energy production and revenue from offshore mining; this would strengthen its financial state.

2. Job Creation and Industrial Growth
   Thousands of jobs can be created in many different ways. Mining, oil extraction and tourism are all examples. This is essential as Sudan holds high unemployment.

3. Infrastructure Development
   Both countries can invest in highways, ports, and logistics infrastructure to support trade and

industrial expansion. Port Sudan could boost
regional connectivity.

4. Strengthening Bilateral and Regional Trade
Joint projects and trade agreements as an outcome
from Red Sea resources can enhance Sudan-Saudi
ties. This enhancement can integrate Sudan further
into the Gulf Cooperation Council (GCC) economic
network.

The Importance of the Red Sea Treasures in the Post-Era of Sudan's Reconstruction

Sudan has endured many years of political instability, but
the post-reconstruction phase presents an opportunity to
leverage its maritime resources for national recovery.

The Red Sea's wealth can contribute to Sudan's economic
revival in several key ways:

1. Strengthening Sudan's Economic Independence
Sudan can reduce its reliance on exports such
as agriculture and improve its foreign exchange
reserves to stabilize the economy.

2. Attracting Foreign Investment
Sudan can position itself as an attractive
investment opportunity, particularly for Gulf and
Asian partners.

3. Enhancing Energy Security
Sudan addressing its energy shortages with the
help of offshore oil and gas extraction could help
reduce dependency on expensive fuel imports. This
also lowers production costs for industries.

4. Supporting Post-War Development
    Revenues generated can be reinvested into
    healthcare, education, and infrastructure, creating
    a sustainable pathway for long-term development.

    The treasures of the Red Sea represent an untapped
    economic goldmine with the potential to reshape
    the future of both nations. The 1974 Agreement is
    a foundation for collaboration, it ensures equitable
    resource sharing and long-term sustainability.
    For Sudan, especially in the context of post-
    war reconstruction, these resources provide an
    opportunity to attract investments, diversify the
    economy and rebuild national infrastructure.

    As technology advances and dynamics shift, both
    nations must adopt sustainable and cooperative
    strategies to fully utilise the benefits of their shared
    maritime wealth. By doing so, Sudan and Saudi
    Arabia can unlock a new era of prosperity and
    stability in the Red Sea region.

Why Should Sudan Engage in Establishing a Nuclear Project for Peaceful Purposes in the Post-War Era?

In the post-war era, Sudan faces the critical task of
rebuilding its key institutions, economy and infrastructure.
Establishing a nuclear programme for peaceful purposes
can play an important role in the process by providing
sustainable energy, enhancing economic development, and
strengthening scientific and technological capabilities.

Below are the key reasons why Sudan should pursue a peaceful nuclear project:

1. Energy Security and Sustainable Development
    – There is an increasing demand for energy, to support the economic recovery.
    – Reliable, sustainable and long-term energy sources can be taken from nuclear power.
    – Relying and depending less on fossil fuels and imported energy can aid in stabilizing the energy costs and enhance national energy security.
    – Alignment with global efforts to transform into low carbon energy sources, navigating climate change consequences.

2. Economic Growth and Industrial Development
    – Foreign investment and partnerships can be attracted via a nuclear energy programme.
    – Stimulation of industrial growth through consistent power to agricultural and manufacturing industries.
    – Creation of high-skilled job and career opportunities for engineers, scientists and technicians.

3. Advancement in Science, Technology, and Education
    – The establishment of a nuclear programme will inspire research in nuclear physics, engineering, and medical applications.
    – The enhancement of Sudan's scientific and technological expertise. Fostering innovation and modernization.

- Providing training, technical support, knowledge transfer through the collaboration with international nuclear agencies.

4. Medical and Agricultural Benefits
   - Nuclear technology has benefits in medicine. Cancer treatments that are done through radiation therapy and advanced diagnostic tools are both examples.
   - Agricultural benefits: for food preservation, pest control, and improving crop yields through radiation-based techniques.

5. Water Resource Management
   - Water scarcity and desertification is a real issue and challenge in Sudan.
   - Desalination projects could use nuclear tech to provide fresh water for drinking and irrigation.

6. Strengthening International Relations and Cooperation
   - A peaceful nuclear programme will provide Sudan the opportunity to engage with international organizations and global scientific communities.
   - It can create diplomatic relations with nations that have advanced nuclear programmes, leading to broader economic and technological cooperation.

7. Compliance with International Safety and Non-Proliferation Standards
   - A peaceful nuclear programme must align with international safety protocols to ensure security and environmental protection.

- Engaging in peaceful nuclear activities. Within the scope of the framework of the International Atomic Energy Agency (IAEA).

Establishment and implementation of a peaceful nuclear programme could be a great step for Sudan in its post-war recovery. It would allow for a stable energy source, drive economic growth, enhance scientific research, and contribute to overall national development. Sudan must ensure there exist proper regulatory frameworks, international cooperation, and investment in human capital to implement such a project safely and effectively.

Post-War Era: Why Should Sudan Explore and Adopt Joint Defence Agreements?

In the post-war era, Sudan should seriously consider the exploration and adaptation of joint defence agreements to strengthen national security, promote regional stability, and benefit from military and strategic cooperation with partner nations.

Here are the key reasons why such agreements would be beneficial:

1. Strengthening National Security
   - Sudan is located in an area that faces many security threats, including border disputes, terrorism, arms trafficking, and non-state armed groups. Joint defence agreements can provide technical and military support to counter these challenges effectively.

2. Building Advanced Military Capabilities
   - Modernization of armed forces. Key methods include knowledge exchange and joint training exercises with allied countries.
   - Technology transfers and the development of a national defence industry could be included in the agreements.

3. Promoting Regional Stability
   - De-escalate border tensions and building of trust through defence cooperation with neighbouring countries.
   - Security agreements within the Horn of Africa or the Arab League, could contribute to long-term stability in the region.

4. Reducing Dependence on Foreign Powers
   - The establishment of regional defence partnerships can reduce dependence on foreign interventions for security.
   - Defence diplomacy can aid Sudan in maintaining its sovereignty while engaging in strategic partnerships.

5. Enhancing Sudan's International Standing
   - Signing defence agreements with key regional and global players can improve Sudan's diplomatic position.
   - These agreements may also bring political and economic support through bilateral partnerships and strategic cooperation.

Challenges to Consider

- Preventing entanglement in international or regional conflicts through the establishment of defence agreements.
- Alliances that do not compromise national sovereignty.
- Balancing national interests with the obligations that come with joint defence commitments.

What Are Sudan's Options?

- Joining Regional Defence Alliances: Such as the African Union's Peace and Security Council.
- Signing Bilateral Defence Agreements.
- Strengthening Cooperation with the UN and AU: To take part in peacekeeping operations and regional security initiatives.

If Sudan implements these defence agreements, it can improve its security, stability, and role in regional and global peace efforts.

The Post-War Era in Sudan: Importance and Advantages of Establishing a Future Generations Fund (FGF)

After a long time of conflict, Sudan faces the grave challenge of rebuilding its economy, stabilizing its governance, and ensuring sustainable development for future generations.

Establishing a Future Generations Fund (FGF) can be a crucial step in securing long-term stability and prosperity.

Below are its key importance and advantages:

1. Importance of an FGF in Sudan's Post-War aspect
   - Ensuring Economic Stability: Wars deplete resources, create fiscal instability and disrupt industries. An FGF would help stabilize the economy by ensuring long-term savings and investment.
   - Preservation of Wealth for Future Generations: Sudan's natural resources, especially oil, gold, and agriculture, need to be efficiently maintained. An FGF ensures that the benefits of these resources are saved and invested for future generations.
   - Attracting Foreign Investment: A well-structured sovereign wealth fund signals economic stability and good governance, making Sudan more attractive to investors.
   - Mitigating Resource Dependence: The economy is heavily dependent on commodities like gold and oil, which are subject to price volatility. The fund can act as a buffer to stabilize government revenues.
   - Financing Reconstruction and Development: Post-war recovery needs large investments in infrastructure, education, healthcare, and job creation. An FGF can help finance this sustainably.

2. Advantages of Establishing a Future Generations Fund
   - Wealth Accumulation for Long-Term Prosperity
   - By investing some of national revenue in global assets, the wealth of the nation can be

improved and financial security can be ensured for generations to come.
- Macroeconomic Stability and Crisis Management
- The fund can serve as a reserve during economic crises, aiding Sudan in the management of currency depreciation, inflation and economic downturns.
- Reduction of Corruption and Mismanagement
- Mechanisms that are designed accurately with full transparency, can lead to FGF aiding in the reduction of the misuse of public funds by ensuring structured financial management and accountability.
- Supporting Human Development
- Revenues from the fund can be allocated to education, healthcare, and technological innovation, ensuring long-term human capital development.
- Preventing "Resource Curse"
- Many resource-rich nations suffer from economic instability and mismanagement. A well-managed FGF can prevent heavy dependence on volatile resource revenues.
- Strengthening National Unity and Social Welfare
- Making sure that the benefits of national wealth are distributed fairly across regions and generations can contribute to social stability and national unity.

A Future Generations Fund (FGF) is a tool that Sudan can utilize as a method of transitioning from post-war recovery to long-term success. By ensuring economic diversity, fiscal discipline, and wealth preservation, Sudan can safeguard its future and provide sustainable development. The fund's success will depend on strong governance, transparency, and responsible management to prevent misallocation and corruption.

Post-War Challenge in Sudan: Writing Off Foreign Debt

One of the post-war challenges the nation will face is the writing off of debt. This is an essential step towards economic stabilization, rebuilding the country and attracting investments.

This challenge can be analysed from several perspectives:

1. The Scale of Debt and Its Impact on the Economy
   - Sudan has a burden of external debt exceeding $50 billion, owed primarily to international financial institutions and creditor nations. This debt severely cripples development. A large part of the country's revenue is allocated to servicing interest payments instead of funding infrastructure projects and public services.

2. Obstacles to Debt Relief
   - Political Instability: Political stability is a requirement for financial institutions and creditors to approve debt cancellation.
   - Low Credit Rating: Poor credit rating makes it impossible for concessional loans, complicating debt restructuring initiatives.
   - Incomplete Economic Reforms: Sudan had initiated an economic reform programme with the International Monetary Fund (IMF);

however, the war disrupted the progress,
making donors hesitant to offer assistance.

3. Possible Mechanisms for Debt Cancellation
   - Heavily Indebted Poor Countries (HIPC)
     Initiative: Sudan was on track to qualify for this
     before the war. However, the ongoing conflict
     and instability hindered its progression.
   - Bilateral and Multilateral Negotiations:
     Engaging creditor nations, the Paris Club, and
     international organizations to negotiate partial
     or full debt forgiveness.
   - Leveraging Natural Resources and Strategic
     Partnerships: Sudan can use its vast natural
     resources (such as gold and oil) as a basis
     for negotiating debt swaps or economic
     cooperation agreements.

4. The Role of International Support
   - To write off the debt, Sudan will need good
     diplomatic relations, to completely reform the
     economy, and guarantees of long-term stability.
     International partners, including the United
     Nations, IMF, World Bank, and African Union,
     could play a critical role in supporting Sudan's
     post-war economic recovery.

Without debt relief, Sudan risks economic stagnation,
making reconstruction and development difficult.

Implementing a federal system in Sudan is considered
an optimal solution for several reasons:

1. Managing Diversity and Promoting Unity:

Sudan's vast geographic expanse and its multiple levels of diversity, religious, ethnic, linguistic and historical make it a good candidate for federal governance. Federalism can serve as a means to accommodate, promoting unity while respecting regional differences.

2. Enhancing Local Governance and Service Delivery: Decentralizing power allows local governments to address the needs of their communities. Local authorities are often better positioned to respond to the unique challenges and preferences of their populations.

3. Preventing Over-Concentration of Power: A federal structure helps prevent the over-concentration of power in a central authority, which can lead to abuses in regions. By distributing power across levels of government, federalism promotes checks and reduces the risk of authoritarianism.

4. Facilitating Conflict Resolution: Federalism can allow the recognition and accommodating of ethnic, linguistic and cultural diversity. Granting autonomy to diverse groups allows self-governance through regional institutions while sharing power at the national level.

5. Promoting Economic Development: More equitable resource distribution and economic development can arise from decentralizing governance. Regions can tailor their economic

policies to local conditions, fostering innovation and addressing disparities more effectively.

In summary, implementing a federal system in Sudan offers a pathway to manage its complex diversity, enhance governance, prevent power centralization, resolve conflicts, and promote balanced economic development.

Post-War National Reconciliation in Sudan

Post-war national reconciliation in Sudan is a complicated challenge that requires addressing the root causes of conflict, to make sure there is transitional justice, and rebuild trust among communities. Sudan has suffered ongoing conflicts, such as the civil wars between the north and south, as well as conflicts in Darfur, South Kordofan, and Blue Nile.

Key Challenges to National Reconciliation

1. Lack of Trust
   Years of conflict and wars have led to deep divisions and hostilities.

2. External Interference
   Regional and international actors often influence Sudan's conflicts as they complicate peace efforts.

3. Transitional Justice
   There needs to be accountability for the human rights violations and the war crimes committed.

4. Economic and Social Devastation
   Years of war have damaged the infrastructure and
   the economy, making rebuilding a top priority.

5. Ethnic and Cultural Diversity
   Sudan is home to many different ethnic and
   cultural groups that require an inclusive approach
   to governance and reconciliation.

Steps Toward National Reconciliation

1. Inclusive Peace Dialogues
   Bringing everybody together to negotiate a long-
   term peace agreement. (Political groups, armed
   movements, tribes and civil society.)

2. Transitional Justice Mechanisms
   Implementing reconciliation commissions,
   compensation programmes and war crimes
   tribunals for victims.

3. Disarmament, Demobilization, and Reintegration
   (DDR)
   Ensuring former combatants are aided in order
   to reintegrate into society through economic
   opportunities and rehabilitation programmes.

4. Economic Recovery and Development
   Investing in war-stricken areas through the
   rebuilding of infrastructure, job creation, and
   public services.

5. Decentralized Governance and Power-Sharing
    Addressing marginalization, having fair political
    representation and autonomy for diverse areas.

6. Civic Education and Social Cohesion Initiatives
    Promoting dialogue, cultural exchange programmes,
    and educational reforms to create unity.

If reconciliation is to succeed, it should be an inclusive
and sustained process, backed by domestic political will and
international support alike.

The Path Forward: Everyone Has a Role to Play

Rebuilding is a national mission that requires the dedication
of everyone.

To the politicians: Lead with vision and serve the people
with integrity.

-   To the business community: Invest in Sudan, drive
    innovation and create jobs.
-   To the students and young professionals: Seek
    knowledge, build skill sets, and become future
    leaders.
-   To the Sudanese diaspora: Bring investment,
    expertise and ideas back home.
-   To the international community: Support Sudan
    through investment and fair trade and diplomatic
    engagement.

Everyone should ask themselves: What can I do to
contribute in rebuilding my country?

The answer to this question will determine Sudan's future.

Sudan's Choice: A Legacy of Despair or a Future of Hope?

Sudan has an opportunity to become a leader in Africa and the world. However, transformation requires courage, commitment, and sacrifice.

The time for waiting is over. The time for action is now.

Sudan, this is your moment.

Will you seize it?

THE BIRTH OF A RESURGENT SUDAN: A NATION'S LAST CHANCE

Sudan is at the edge of a defining moment in its history. It stands between two different futures: chaos, collapse and conflict or renewal, prosperity and global leadership.

This is the last chance Sudan has to rise. For decades, Sudan has wasted its potential, broken promises, and dreams have been unfulfilled. It is a nation rich in resources but poor in management. Strong in people, weak in leadership. Blessed with opportunities, but cursed with instability. Sudan has seen coups, peace deals, wars, revolutions yet never a long-term transformation. Sudan needs to rebuild itself now, or risk permanent failure.

This book has given an uncompromising vision as well as tools for implementation for the future of Sudan. Solutions are clear, resources exist and the people are ready. A Marshall Plan for the reconstruction of Sudan.

Does Sudan have the will to act upon this plan – that is the real question.

Sudan That Could Have Been And Sudan That Must Be

Imagine a Sudan where:

- Its fertile lands lead Sudan to become the largest agricultural exporter in Africa.
- Its industries produce goods that are considered competition in global markets.
- Its youth are educated, innovative, and drivers and leaders in technology and development.
- Its cities are modern hubs of business, community and culture, thriving.
- Its government is honest, accountable, and works for the benefit of the people.
- Its people, once divided, stand together under one national vision.

This is not a fantasy, this is a real future within reach. Other nations have achieved it, and Sudan can too. But this vision will not happen by itself. It requires sacrifice, determination, and leadership at every level of society.

Because if Sudan fails to act now, the alternative is terrifying:

- A country that is divided.
- A nation trapped in poverty.
- Millions fleeing their own homeland, never to return.
- An entire generation lost to ignorance, hunger, and despair.

Sudan has one final chance to escape this fate. If it fails now, history will not forgive it.

No One Is Coming to Save Sudan – It Must Save Itself

For years, Sudan has looked to the international community for aid and rescue. It has depended on peacekeepers and debt relief. However, no nation has ever become great by begging others for help.

- No one will rebuild Sudan except the Sudanese people.
- No one will fight corruption except those who refuse to tolerate it.
- No one will create jobs except the country's own.
- No one will unite Sudan except its citizens who choose unity.

The world may offer aid, but Sudan's future is in its own hands.

The Final Call: Who Will Stand for Sudan?

This is not just another political moment, this is an existential moment. Sudan will either rise as one nation or fall apart into endless suffering.

The coming years will reveal Sudan's destiny for the next century. Those who lead today will either be remembered as the visionaries who saved their nation, or as those who let it collapse.

So now, the call is clear:
- Who among the leaders will step forward with courage, wisdom, and integrity?

- Who among the youth will dedicate their lives to building?
- Who among the businesses will invest in the country?
- Who among Sudan's citizens will reject division?

History will judge this generation. It will either be remembered as the one that saved Sudan or the one that lost it forever.

The future is waiting for Sudan; are you going to rise or will you simply fall?

Relevant Resources

The following list of reference books and reports provides essential statistical data and relevant information on Sudan's major productive and service sectors, as discussed in this book.

1. Agricultural Resources and Strategies

The **Arab Organization for Agricultural Development** has published a series of annual reports that comprehensively cover agricultural resources, national agricultural strategies, and food security. Key publications include:

- *Permanent Programme for the Sustainability of Arab Food Security* (**2020**)
- *The Strategy of Arab Agricultural Sustainability* **2020–2030**
- *The Arab Food Security Report* (**2023**)

https://www.aoad.org/ASSY43/statbook43Cont.htm

2. National Economic and Resource Data

For detailed insights into Sudan's natural resource sectors, please refer to the **World Bank's** national data reports, available at:

https://www.worldbank.org/en/search?q=Sudan

3. Climate Change and Environmental Impact

A current review of the short- and long-term impacts of climate change on Sudan's national landscape can be found at:

https://climateknowledgeportal.worldbank.org/country/sudan

4. Sudan's Compliance with the African Union Agenda 2063

A comprehensive report evaluating Sudan's governmental efforts and compliance with the strategic development goals outlined in the African Union's *Agenda 2063* is accessible at:

https://www.nepad.org/agenda2063-report/sudan-agenda-2063-report

5. For a comprehensive strategic vision, refer to *Sudan 2025: The Correction of the Path and the Dream for the Future* by **Prof. Kamil Idris**, published in Arabic by **Dar Alsalam Printing and Publishing**, Cairo, Egypt (2016).

https://www.profkamilidris.co.uk/page/about-kamil-idris/

CURRICULUM VITAE

PROFESSOR
DR. KAMIL IDRIS

Former Director General (elected by the Coordination Committee and the General Assembly)

World Intellectual Property Organization (WIPO),
United Nations Specialised Agency

Former Secretary-General (elected by the Council)

International Union for the Protection of New Varieties of
Plants (UPOV)

Former Member (elected by the United Nations General Assembly)

United Nations International Law Commission (ILC)

Former Ambassador
Former President

World Arbitration and Mediation Court (WAMC)

Member

Permanent Court of Arbitration (PCA),
The Hague

President

The International Court of Arbitration and Mediation
(ICAM)

Chairman

Board of Trustees of the Union of the Afro-Asian
Universities

Academic Distinctions

LLB (Law), University of Khartoum (Honors)

Bachelor of Arts, Philosophical Studies, University of Cairo
(Honors)

Diploma, Public Administration (Management
Department), Institute of Public Administration, Khartoum

Master in International Affairs (MAIA), University of Ohio,
USA (First Class Average)

Doctorate (PhD) in International Law, Graduate Institute
of International Studies, University of Geneva (Distinction)

Doctorate Thesis: "Case study on the Treaty Establishing a Preferential Trade Area for Eastern and Southern African States"

Academic Interests

Certificates

- International Economics, Graduate Institute of International Studies (Geneva)
- International History and Political Science, Graduate Institute of International Studies (Geneva)
- International Law of Development, Graduate Institute of International Studies (Geneva)
- The Law of International Waterways, Graduate Institute of International Studies (Geneva)
- International Law of Financing and Banking Systems, Graduate Institute of International Studies (Geneva)

Languages

- Arabic, English, French, Spanish (good knowledge)

Teaching

- Lecturer in Philosophy and Jurisprudence,
- University of Cairo (1976-1977)
- Lecturer in Jurisprudence, Ohio University, USA (1978)
- External Examiner in International Law, Faculty of Law, University of Khartoum (1984)
- Lecturer in Intellectual Property Law, Faculty of Law, University of Khartoum (1986)

- Lecturer in several international, regional and national seminars, workshops and symposia
- Member, International Association for the Advancement of Teaching and Research in Intellectual Property Law (ATRIP)

Decorations

- Awarded the Scholars and Researchers State Gold Medal, presented by the President of the Republic of the Sudan (1983)
- Awarded the Scholars and Researchers Gold Medal, presented by the President of the Academy of Scientific Research and Technology of Egypt (1985)
- Awarded the decoration of the Commandeur de l'Ordre national du Lion, Senegal (1998)
- Awarded the Medal of the Bolshoi Theatre, presented by the Director of the Bolshoi Theatre, Russian Federation (1999)
- Awarded the Honorary Medal, presented by the Rector of the Moscow State Institute of International Relations, Russian Federation (1999)
- Awarded the Honorary Medal of The Gulf Cooperation Council (GCC), Saudi Arabia (1999)
- Awarded the Golden Plaque of the Town of Banská Bystrica, presented by the Mayor of Banská Bystrica, Slovakia (1999)
- Awarded the Golden Medal of Matej Bel University, presented by the Dean of the University, Banská Bystrica, Slovakia (1999)
- Awarded the Silver Jubilee Medal of the Eurasian Patent Organization (EAPO), presented by Mr. Viktor Blinnikov, President of the Eurasian Patent Office, Russian Federation (2000)

- Award of Distinguished Merit, presented by the Egyptian Supreme Council for Science and Technology, Egypt (2000)
- Awarded a Plaque from the Syrian Inventors' Association, Syrian Arab Republic (2000)
- Awarded the Grand Cross of the Infante D. Enrique, Portugal (2001)
- Awarded a Medal from the People's Assembly of Egypt, Egypt (2001)
- Awarded a Medal from the Constitutional Court of Romania, Romania (2001)
- Awarded a Medal from the Parliament of Romania, Romania (2001)
- Awarded the Golden Medal Dolores del Río al Mérito internacional en favor de los derechos de los artistas intérpretes from the National Association of Interpreters (ANDI), Mexico (2001)
- Awarded the Golden Medal from The State Agency on Industrial Property Protection, Republic of Moldova (2001)
- Awarded the decoration of the Commandeur de l'Ordre du Mérite national, Côte d'Ivoire (2002)
- Awarded the Maria Sklodowska-Curie Medal from the Association of Polish Inventors and Rationalizers, Poland (2002)
- Awarded the decoration of The Order of the Two Niles, First Class, from the President of the Republic of Sudan, Sudan (2002)
- Kamil Idris Library, University of Juba, Sudan (2002)
- Kamil Idris Conference Hall, Intellectual Property Court, The Judiciary, Sudan (2002)
- Awarded the Dank Medal (medal of glory), from the President of the Kyrgyz Republic, Kyrgyzstan (2003)

- Award from the University of National and World Economy, Bulgaria (2003)
- "Venice Award for Intellectual Property", presented by the Mayor of Venice (2004)
- Awarded the Medal of Oman, presented by His Royal Highness Fahid Bin Mahmud Al-Said, Deputy Prime Minister of the Council of Ministers, Oman (2004)
- Awarded the decoration of the Aztec Eagle, presented by Ambassador Luis Alfonso de Alba (Permanent Representative of Mexico to International Organizations in Geneva) on behalf of Presidente of Mexico Vicente Fox, (2005)
- Kamil Idris Building, Regional Training Center, African Regional Intellectual Property Organization (ARIPO), Harare, Zimbabwe (2006)
- Awarded a Medal commemorating the 60 years of the United Nations, Bulgaria (2006)
- Awarded a Medal commemorating the 60 years of the Independence of Jordan, Jordan (2006)
- Award of Distinguished Leadership presented by the International Publishers' Association (IPA) and the Arab Publishers Association, Egypt (2007)
- Awarded a Medal on the occasion of the Fujairah International Monodrama Festival, Fujairah,United Arab Emirates (2007)
- Awarded a Medal on the occasion of the Intellectual Property Day presented by The Regional Institute for Intellectual Property of the Faculty of Law, University of Helwan, Egypt (2008)
- Awarded The Distinguished Medal of Cultural Innovation, Sudan (2008)
- Awarded The Family Club Decoration, Sudan (2008)
- Awarded The World Intellectual Property Organization (WIPO) Medal, Geneva, Switzerland(2008)

- Awarded The International Union Of The Protection Of New Varieties Of Plants (UPOV)
- Medal, Geneva, Switzerland (2008)
- Awarded The Distinguished Medal Of The Sudanese Centre Of Intellectual Property, Khartoum, Sudan (2009)
- Awarded The Medal Of Kenana sugar Company, Khartoum , Sudan (2009)
- Awarded The Decoration Of Loyalty And Gratitude Of Omdurman National Broadcasting Station, Sudan (2010)
- Awarded The decoration (WISHAH) of the Syrian revolution (2013)
- Awarded The decoration (WISHAH) of Rashid Diab cultural center, Khartoum , Sudan (2013)
- Awarded The Medal of Distinction by the International Association of Muslim

Lawyers (2014)

Honorary Degrees

- 1999 Honorary Professor of Law, Peking University, China
- 1999 Doctor Honoris Causa, The Doctor's Council of the State University of Moldova, Republic of Moldova
- 1999 Doctor Honoris Causa, Franklin Pierce Law Center (Concord, New Hampshire), United States of America
- 1999 Doctor Honoris Causa, Fudan University (Shanghai), China
- 2000 Doctor Honoris Causa, University of National and World Economy (Sofia), Bulgaria

- 2001 Doctor Honoris Causa, University of Bucharest, Romania
- 2001 Doctor Honoris Causa, Hannam University (Daejeon), Republic of Korea
- 2001 Doctor Honoris Causa, Mongolian University of Science and Technology (Ulaanbaatar), Mongolia
- 2001 Doctor Honoris Causa, Matej Bel University (Banská Bystrica), Slovakia
- 2002 Doctor Honoris Causa, National Technical University of Ukraine "Kyiv Polytechnic Institute" (Kyiv), Ukraine
- 2003 Doctor Honoris Causa, Al Eman Al Mahdi University (White Nile State), Sudan
- 2005 Degree of Doctor of Letters (Honoris Causa), Indira Gandhi National Open University (IGNOU), India
- 2005 Doctor Honoris Causa, Latvian Academy of Sciences, Latvia
- 2006 Doctor Honoris Causa, University of Azerbaijan, Azerbaijan
- 2007 Doctor Honoris Causa, University of Al-Gezira, Sudan
- 2007 Doctor of International Law and Honorary Professor, Belarussian State University, Belarus
- 2007 Doctor Honoris Causa, University of Khartoum, Sudan
- 2007 Doctor Honoris Causa, Ss. Cyril and Methodius University (Skopje), The Former Yugoslav Republic of Macedonia
- 2008 Doctor Honoris Causa, Kyrgyz State University of Construction, Transport and Architecture (Bishkek), Kyrgystan
- 2008 Certificate of Appreciation, Ahlia University, Khartoum, Sudan

- 2020 Honorary Professor, Durham University (United Kingdom)

Experience

Professional

- Part-time Journalist, El-Ayam and El-Sahafa (Sudanese) newspapers (1971-1979)
- Lecturer, University of Cairo (1976)
- Assistant Director, Arab Department, Ministry of Foreign Affairs, Khartoum (1977)
- Assistant Director, Research Department, Ministry of Foreign Affairs, Khartoum (January-June 1978)
- Deputy Director, Legal Department, Ministry of Foreign Affairs, Khartoum (July-December 1978)
- Member of Sudan Permanent Mission to the United Nations Office, Geneva (1979-1982)
- Vice-Consul of Sudan in Switzerland (1979-1982)
- Legal Adviser of Sudan Permanent Mission to the United Nations Office, Geneva (1979-1982)
- Senior Program Officer, Development Cooperation and External Relations Bureau for Africa, World Intellectual Property Organization (WIPO), (1982-1985)
- Director, Development Cooperation and External Relations Bureau for Arab and Central and Eastern European Countries, WIPO (1985-1994)
- Ambassador, Ministry of Foreign Affairs, Sudan (current status at national level)
- Deputy Director General, WIPO (1994-1997)
- Director General, WIPO, since 1997
- Secretary-General, International Union for the Protection of Plant Varieties (UPOV), since 1997

Special

- External Assessor for the title of Professor, College of Islamic Studies (CIS), Sheikh Hamad University, Doha, Qatar 2024
- Member of The Academic Council, University of Khartoum (Sudan, April 2007)
- Member, Board of Trustees, Nile Valley University (Egypt, June 2000)
- Member, United Nations International Law Commission (ILC) (2000-2001)
- Member, Advisory Council on Intellectual Property (ACIP), Franklin Pierce Law Center (Concord, New Hampshire, 1999)
- Member, United Nations International Law Commission (ILC) (1992-1996)
- Vice-Chairman of the International Law Commission (ILC) at its 45th session (1993)
- Representative of the ILC in the 35th session of the Asian-African Legal Consultative Committee (AALCC) (Manila, March 1996)
- Member, Working Group of the ILC on the drafting of the Statute of the International Criminal Court
- Member, Drafting Committee of the ILC
- Legal expert in a number of Ministerial Committees between Sudan and other countries
- Member of the Legal Experts Committee of the Organization of African Unity (OAU), which formulated several regional conventions
- Legal adviser in the Ministerial Councils and the Summit Conferences of the OAU (Khartoum, July 1978) (Monrovia, July 1979)
- Participant in several meetings and international conferences of WHO, ILO, ITU, WIPO, Red Cross and

the Executive Committee of the High Commissioner for Refugees
- Member of Special Committees established for fundraising for refugees in Africa
- Rapporteur of the Third Committee (Marine Scientific Research) of the summary Ninth session of the Third UN Conference on the Law of the Sea (Geneva, 1980)
- Head of Sudan Delegation to the OAU Preparatory Meeting on the Draft Code of Conduct on Transfer of Technology (Addis Ababa, March 1981)
- Spokesman of the African Group and the Group of 77 on all issues pertaining to Transfer of Technology, Energy, Restrictive Business Practices and Technical Co-operation among Developing Countries at the twenty-second and twenty-third sessions of the Trade and Development Board (Geneva, February and September 1981
- Head of Sudan Delegation and Spokesman of the African Group and Coordinator of the Group of 77 at the fourth session of the UN Conference on the Code of Conduct on Transfer of Technology (Geneva, March-April 1981)
- Spokesman of the Group of 77 on Chapter 9 (Applicable Law and Settlement of Disputes) at the UN Conference on the International Code of Conduct on Transfer of Technology (Geneva, March-April 1981)
- Head of Sudan Delegation and Chairman of the Workshop on Legal Policies on Technology Transfer (Kuwait, September 1981)
- Chairman of the African Group and the Group of 77 at the first session of the Intergovernmental Group of Experts on Restrictive Business Practices (Geneva, November 1981)
- Chairman of the Permanent Group of 15 on Transfer and Development of Technology, within the United Nations

Conference on Trade and Development (UNCTAD) (Geneva, 1980-1983)
- Spokesman of the African Group and the Group of 77 at the meeting on the Economic, Commercial and Developmental Aspects of the Industrial Property System (Geneva, February 1982)
- Coordinator of the African Group and the Group of 77 at the first, second and third sessions of the Interim Committee on the International Code of Conduct on Transfer of Technology (Geneva, March, May, September-October 1982)
- Coordinator of the African Group and the Group of 77 at the Meeting of Governmental Experts on the Transfer, Application and Development of Technology in the Capital Goods and Industrial Machinery Sectors (Geneva, July 1982)
- Coordinator and spokesman of the African Group and the Group of 77 at the Intergovernmental Group of Experts on the Feasibility of Measuring Human Resource Flows on Reverse Transfer of Technology (Brain-Drain) (Geneva, August-September 1982)
- Coordinator of developing countries on the drafting of the resolution concerning the mandate of the Office of the United Nations High Commissioner for Refugees, during the thirty-third session of the Executive Committee of the UNHCR (Geneva, October 1982)
- Coordinator and spokesman of the African Group and the Group of 77 at the Meeting of Governmental Experts on the Transfer, Application and Development of Technology in the Energy Sector (Geneva, October-November 1982)
- Coordinator and spokesman of the African Group and the Group of 77 at the fourth session of the Committee on Transfer of Technology (Geneva, November-December 1982)

- Member, Board of Patrons, IP Management Resource (On-line version of Intellectual Property/Innovation Management Handbook), 2007
- Co-President, Foreign Relations Committee, Ministry of Culture (Sudan, 2011)
- President, Sudan Foundation for the defense of Syrian people (2012-2013)
- Vice-President, Sudan Foundation for the defense of Rights and Freedom s (2012-2013)
- Member, Sudan Foundation for Reconciliation and Religious co-existence (2012-2013)
- Judicial Experience and Professional Membership of Associations
- Member of the United Nations International Law Commission (ILC) (1992-1996) and (2000-2001)
- Member and Chairman of several legal experts committees established within the OAU
- Professor of Public International Law, University of Khartoum , Sudan
- Member of the Sudan Bar Association (Khartoum)
- Member of the African Jurists Association (Dakar and Paris)
- Alternate Chair, Council of Foreign Relations, Ministry of Culture, Sudan
- Registered Advocate and Commissioner for Oaths in the Republic of Sudan
- Vice President, Sudan Organisation for the Protection of Fundamental Rights and Freedoms
- Member, Sudan High Level Committee on Judicial Reform

Projects and Documents

- Formulated and negotiated, on behalf of WIPO, numerous projects relating to development cooperation in the field of intellectual property

- Organized, on behalf of WIPO, various seminars and workshops and presented several lectures
- Drafted various documents on developmental aspects of intellectual property
- Supervised and managed the administrative and substantive aspects of projects executed worldwide

Conferences, Seminars, Courses and Symposia

- Represented Sudan in numerous international and regional conferences; participated in many seminars, symposia, discussion groups, and addressed graduate students on various international academic disciplines
- Represented WIPO, in various international meetings, seminars and symposia
- Represented WIPO on several UNDP Policy and Operations Programmes
- Undertook a study tour at the Max Planck Institute (Munich) in the field of teaching of intellectual property law (1986)
- Extensive lecture on COVID-19: The legal consequences of contractual obligations (May, 2020)

Publications

- Euro-Arab Dialogue, June 1977
- State Responsibility in International Law, September 1977
- The Theory of Human Action, September 1977
- The Philosophy of "Haddith" and "Sunna" in Islamic Law, January 1978
- The Doctrine of Jurisdiction in International Law, December 1978
- American Embassy in Tehran Case, March 1979

- The Legal Regime of the Nile, December 1980
- Issues pertaining to Transfer and Development of Technology in Sudan, May 1981
- China and the Powers in the 19th Century, May 1981
- Legal Dimensions of the Economic Cooperation among Developing Countries, June 1981
- The Common Fund for Commodities, June 1981
- General Aspects of Transfer of Technology at the National and International Levels, November 1981
- Preferential Trading Arrangements among Developing Countries, February 1982
- North-South Insurance Relations: The Unequal Exchange, December 1984
- The Law of Non-Navigational Uses of International Water Courses; the International Law Commission's draft articles: An overview, November 1995
- The Theory of Source and Target in Child Psychology, January 1996
- A Better United Nations for the New Millennium, January 2000
- Intellectual Property – A Power Tool for Economic Growth, 2003
- Sudan, The Year 2020: Lessons and Visions, 2004
- The Intellectual Property-Conscious Nations: Mapping the Path from Developing to Developed, 2006
- Sudan 2020, (2008)
- Sudan: From Least-Developed to Fast Developing, 2008
- Arbitration: A Vision for the Enforcement of Justice, 2009
- Arbitration: Critical Review Of Sudan Legislation onArbitration (2005), 2009
- A guide to my philosophy and quotations, 2015
- Sudan's Path to the Future: A realistic dream for 2025, 2017

- JASTA and the third World War, 2018
- A Memoir: My Nile Odyssey, 2019
- How: Mind-Set Success, Promise: Nothing Less Than My Dream: 2020
- My Nile Odyssey (Arabic translation): 2022
- JASTA and the third World War (Arabic translation): 2022
- My Nile Odyssey (Audio Book):2023
- DEMYSTIFY: The Unseen Path
- Insights from Moses and Al Khidr: 2024
- The Unseen Path (Arabic translation): 2025
- BEYOND THE VEIL: A METAPHYSICAL ODYSSEY: 2025
- Sudan's Marshall Plan: Rebuilding the World's Forgotten Powerhouse: 2025

Books under publication

WHISPERS OF POWER:
ENCOUNTERS WITH GLOBAL ICONS

VOLCANIC FURY:
THE DEADLY TOLL OF ANGER

SILENT WISDOM:
THE POWER OF SAYING NOTHING

UNIVERSE CONTROLLED:
THE SOVREIGNTY OF ALLAH

DARK SECRETS:
The HIDDEN TRUTHS

HEART's THRONE:
WHY THE MIND IS JUST A PUPPET?

Articles

- A number of articles on law, economics, jurisprudence and aesthetics published in various newspapers and periodicals.
- Russia's Invasion of Crimea: Is it a violation of International Law?

INDEX

www.ingramcontent.com/pod-product-compliance
Lightning Source LLC
Chambersburg PA
CBHW070806280326
41934CB00012B/3078